AFTER THE POGROM

AFTER THE POGROM

7 OCTOBER, ISRAEL AND THE CRISIS OF CIVILISATION

BRENDAN O'NEILL

spiked

First published in 2024 by Spiked Ltd

© Spiked Ltd

Spiked Ltd
c/o Sierra Quebec Bravo
7th Floor, 77 Marsh Wall
London, E14 9SH
www.spiked-online.com

A catalogue record for this book is available from the British Library.

ISBN: 978-1-0687193-0-1

Requests to publish works from this book should be sent to Viv Regan, viv.regan@spiked-online.com

Cover design: Alex Dale
Typesetting: Vivian Head

CONTENTS

INTRODUCTION

8 October 2023 ought to have been a day of shining moral clarity for humankind. In the preceding 24 hours, something terrible had occurred. Something almost unimaginable. A thing that felt like it belonged to the last century, to the century of war and extermination, intruded into ours. Atavistic hatreds leapt from the pages of the history books. An orgy of killing of the kind we had previously only seen in black-and-white photos and sanitised Hollywood films unfolded in real time. The past invaded the present. The pogrom returned.

Hamas and other Islamist groups invaded Israel to murder Jews. They moved with extreme prejudice through the kibbutzim and deserts of the south of Israel. No one was spared. Not children, not women, not the elderly. Rockets were fired at moving cars. Grenades were thrown into bomb shelters in which families had taken refuge. A music festival was turned into a slaughter zone. What had been a joyous gathering of youths under the spell of trance music became a site of rape and murder. Three hundred and sixty-four souls were extinguished there.

The numbers are grim. More than 1,100 people were killed in total, 796 of them civilians. Two hundred and fifty were taken hostage. They included three-year-old twins and an 85-year-old grandmother. Yet even the death toll, much as it chills the soul, fails to capture the full horror of the day. It was the sadism of the violence, the glee in it, that ought to have awoken the world's conscience. They filmed their barbarism and shared it online. They took pride in their bloodbath. One pogromist phoned home to boast to his parents about how many Jews he had killed.

They dragged their bruised, bloodied hostages back to Gaza and paraded them in the streets. The broken body of a young woman who had been raving just hours earlier was jeered at, spat on, beaten with sticks. It echoed the annihilations of old. A violence we no longer thought possible, the pogrom we thought was the stuff of museums, brutally imprinted itself on our complacent century. Hamas had fulfilled the promise of its founding covenant, which was to kill Jews.

This was more than terrorism. It was more than mass murder. It was a 'total derailment from civilisation', in the words of German novelist Herta Müller. The Jewish nation found itself subjected to the very butchery it was built to withstand. The state to which Jews fled to escape the pogroms was now besieged by a pogrom. It felt like the most grave of violations, both of the sanctuary of the Jews and of the pact humankind made in the aftermath of the last great war: Never Again.

And yet that shining moral clarity never came. Israel waited in vain for the young and the educated of the West to rally to its side. Few here seemed to appreciate the enormity of what had occurred, the challenge it posed not only to the Jewish State, but also to humanity in its entirety. Hamas had not only tested Israel's territorial security, but also mankind's moral conscience. It laid down a gauntlet alongside its grenades. It dared us to pit our civilisation against its barbarism. It dared us to be decisive. And we failed.

The lucidity of moral thought that this atrocious moment called for was shockingly absent. The marshalling of the human spirit against the pogromists failed to materialise. The world's conscience slept. Instead, people talked about 'context', as if there could ever be a context for fascist murder. People said it was Israel's own fault for mistreating the Palestinians, as if a pogrom is a legitimate response to grievance. People made excuses for evil.

Worse, people celebrated. In the immediate aftermath of the carnage, people took to the streets of London, Berlin, Sydney – not to sympathise with the Jews but to laud their killers. 'Fuck the Jews', they said in Sydney. 'I support the attack 100 per cent', said a protester in London. 'Long live 7 October', said a banner in New York City. Sympathy for Hamas exploded on our campuses, admiration for its terror was hollered on our streets. A dawning, chilling realisation came: too many had taken up the cause not of the Jews, but of their persecutors.

7 October was primarily a day of horror and grief for Israelis. It was the worst attack the modern State of Israel has experienced in its 76 years of existence. But it was a moral test, too. It was a moral test for the world. Many books will be written about the Israel-Hamas War and the future of Israel after 7 October. But that's what this book is about – why we failed this moral test, and what we might do to ensure we never fail a test like this again.

ONE

THE LURE OF BARBARISM

There were two eruptions of barbarism in October 2023. The first was Hamas's pogrom of 7 October, in which more than a thousand people were slaughtered and many others maimed, raped and kidnapped. The second was the sympathy for the pogrom across much of the Western world. The excuse-making for Hamas's atrocities. The celebration, even, of this army of anti-Semites that had paraglided, barged and driven into southern Israel to decimate the civilian population there. The bodies were barely cold, the hostages not yet shackled in Gaza's dank tunnels, the rape victims still reeling from their vile defilement, when a cruel, taunting cry came from the West: 'Well, what did you expect?'

On campuses, on social media and on the streets, there was an explosion of empathy – not with Israel but with the extremist brutes who had just so horrifically violated its territory and its people. Leftists, influencers and members of the educated elites issued apologias for Hamas's butchery of civilians. Some outright crowed about it. It was 'exhilarating' and 'energising', said one American professor of Hamas's incursion.[1] 'Glory to our martyrs', said students at George Washington University in Washington, DC.[2] A leading political theorist wrote about the thrill some felt upon seeing images of 'paragliders evading Israeli air defences' and carrying out 'seemingly impossible acts of bravery'.[3] What exactly is brave about blinding children with hand grenades and kidnapping grandmothers is anyone's guess.[4]

For some Western radicals, the image of the paragliding pogromist became iconic. The Chicago chapter of Black Lives Matter tweeted an image of a paraglider alongside the slogan: 'I stand with Palestine.'[5] Here was a movement that had spent the past 10 years protesting against racism now slyly gloating over one of the worst acts of racist violence of modern times. Soon, Hamas cosplay became a thing. Men in Hamas-style green bandanas were spotted on one of the anti-Israel marches in London.[6] Also in London, three young women were photographed sporting paraglider stickers.[7] They were later arrested and convicted of expressing support for terrorism.[8] In the weeks following Hamas's orgy of murder, legions of England's middle classes idly marched alongside radical Islamists who were chanting for 'jihad' – that is, holy war – against the Jewish State. One pogrom wasn't enough, it seems.

The true extent of Western sympathy for Hamas in the aftermath of its apocalyptic assault on the Jews of southern Israel was made clear in opinion polls.[9] Among the young in particular, affinity with Hamas and its ugly aims seemed chillingly commonplace. In December 2023, a Harvard / Harris poll found that 60 per cent of American 18- to 24-year-olds believed Hamas's attack was justified by Palestinian grievances. An alarming 50 per cent said they sided with Hamas against Israel. And 51 per cent said they favoured a one-state solution in which the Jewish State would be brought to an end and the land handed to Hamas and the Palestinians.[10] There's a phrase for that: ethnic cleansing. Here we had 'radical' youths who one minute were protesting against Israel's supposed ethnic cleansing in Gaza, and the next were dreaming of ridding the Middle East entirely of the Jewish State and granting dominion to known Jew-haters instead.

We need to talk about this. We need to talk about the pity for the pogromists that swept the West in the wake of 7 October. We need to talk about the exhilaration of the educated classes upon seeing kibbutzim invaded and Jews' homes set on fire. We need to talk about the left's rationalisation of the pogrom. We need to talk about the fact that when barbarism visited Israel, when fascism reared its head once more, many of our young took its side. It won't do to write off all this Hamasmania as the handiwork of a few hotheaded Israel-haters. As leftist commentator Leigh Phillips argues, it isn't true that the 'paraglider left' is just a 'handful of fringe idiots': no, 'the phenomenon is too widespread to ignore'.[11]

It is. We can no longer ignore the Western response to Hamas's pogrom. We can no longer ignore the fact that even the worst act of violence against the Jews since the Holocaust was not enough to awaken the West to the threat posed by radical Islam – not only to the Jewish State, but also to the West itself. The first eruption of barbarism in October 2023 – Hamas's carnival of killing – confirmed what many of us already knew about Hamas: that it is a Jew-hating war machine that masquerades as a national-liberation movement. The second eruption of barbarism – the pogrom apologism that so swiftly infected our own cities and institutions – surely confirms the moral disarray of a Western world that has turned its back on the principles of the Enlightenment and the virtues of civilisation. Ignoring this would be nothing short of suicidal.

It is imperative that we revisit the madness that seized the West in the weeks and months after Hamas's pogrom. Even when the pogrom was ongoing, even as old men were being shot in their living rooms and music-festival attendees were being shoved on to trucks, there were expressions of political glee at what one commentator romanticised as a mass prison break. '[The] people of Gaza had broken out of their prison', we were told, and it was something to celebrate.[12]

Literally. Today is 'a day of celebration', said Rivkah Brown of the British left-wing outlet, Novara Media, on 7 October itself.[13] She cheered the crossing of 'Hamas fighters... into their colonisers' territory'. To those who were already raising concerns about Hamas's targeting of civilians, Brown said: 'The struggle for freedom is rarely bloodless and we shouldn't apologise for it.' Her colleague Michael Walker rhetorically asked: 'Do we support the rights of an occupied people to fight an occupier or not?' Novara contributor and senior lecturer at Birkbeck University in London, Ashok Kumar, tweeted: 'Sometimes partying on stolen land next to a concentration camp where a million people are starved has consequences.' He was referring to Hamas's assault on the Nova music festival during its pogrom. Where it massacred 364 partying youths. And gang-raped women. And mutilated others.[14] Calling such murderous brutality a 'consequence' of holding a festival in the south of Israel is an underhand way of saying those people had it coming.

All three walked back their celebratory remarks, when the extent of Hamas's butchery became clearer. And yet that initial instinct to cheer 7 October, to say, essentially, that Israel got what it deserved, was widespread on that day of infamy.

While the pogrom was in full flow, 31 student organisations at Harvard University issued a statement saying 'the Israeli regime' is 'entirely responsible for all unfolding violence'. Israel is 'the only one to blame', decreed these Ivy League radicals. This was the politics of 'She was asking for it'. As women were being raped and ravers murdered, 5,000 miles away, on the peaceful, leafy lawns of Harvard, the sons and daughters of privilege were saying it was their own damned fault. Not the knife-wielders of Hamas. Not that movement's rapists and murderers. No, it was the country in which those men carried out their inhuman deeds that was responsible for it all; for its own suffering; for the sexual degradation of its women and the summary execution of its men.

It was 'victim-blaming' *par excellence*. Harvard radicals are the kind of people who normally wring their hands over 'victim-blaming'. Blaming the victims of injustice for their own predicament is a mortal sin in the eyes of the activist set. Indeed, Harvard Law School has issued advice on 'how to avoid victim-blaming'. It is unconscionable to say 'the victim rather than the perpetrator bears responsibility for [an] assault', it says. And yet that's exactly what those 31 societies at Harvard did. They blamed Israelis for their own murders. They exonerated the pogromists and condemned the pogromists' victims.

Universities were hotbeds of the Hamas sympathy that spread like a virus after the pogrom. The projection of the slogan 'Glory to our martyrs' on to the exterior of a campus building at George Washington University was grim proof of that. It was reportedly the work of the radical group, Students for Justice in Palestine.[15] Here we had the kind of campus that has spent years bemoaning the 'racism' of white kids culturally appropriating black hairstyles, and the 'rape culture' of male students drunkenly propositioning female students, now openly praising the racists and rapists of Hamas.[16] In the warped moral universe of what now passes for the left, a white person eating sushi is racial arrogance, while an army of bigots slaughtering a thousand Jews is glorious martyrdom. Putting your hand on a woman's knee is a #MeToo outrage – violating women *en masse* in the Negev desert is resistance.[17]

At Birmingham University in England, protesters displayed a banner saying 'Zionists off our campus'. Some allegedly chanted 'Death to Zionists'.[18] A similar sentiment was expressed by one of the leading organisers of the pro-Palestine encampment at Columbia University in New York City. 'Zionists don't deserve to live', he said.[19] Shortly after the pogrom, two branches of the UK's University and College Union put forward motions calling for 'intifada until victory'.[20] How were we meant to interpret the word 'intifada' in that context? Just weeks after Hamas had carried out a so-called 'intifada' that entailed the mass slaughter of Jews? To some, it looked like an academic embrace of such visceral violence. It seemed to go 'beyond a plea for Palestinian statehood', wrote Hadley Freeman, and instead came across as 'an explicit threat against Israel and the [Jewish] Diaspora'.[21]

Teachers and professors were often at the forefront of celebrating the pogrom. It was a mere week after 7 October that Cornell University professor Russell Rickford said that, yes, 'horrific acts' were carried out by Hamas, but 7 October was nonetheless 'exhilarating'. 'It was energising', he said. Those who fail to feel stirred by Hamas's actions, by its 'challenge to the monopoly of violence', are not fully human, he insisted.[22]

An Islamic scholar at the University of California, Irvine described 7 October as 'a gift from Allah'. It was a just attack on the 'bloodthirsty animals' of Zionism, he said.[23] A lecturer at the City University of New York called for further resistance against the 'Babylon swine' that are Zionists.[24] A professor at Columbia University, just a day after the pogrom, wrote of the 'jubilation and awe' inspired by the 'storming [of] Israeli checkpoints' by Hamas's 'resistance fighters'. He cheered 'the resistance's remarkable takeover' of facilities in southern Israel.[25] A professor at Albany Law School in New York State celebrated Hamas for 'tearing down the walls of colonialism'.[26] In the UK, a professor at Leicester University described 7 October as 'heroic'.[27] On and on it went, academics awestruck by Hamas, enlivened by barbarism, moved by murder.

Political theorist Jodi Dean summed up the narcissism of these overeducated sympathisers with Hamas. For Verso, a leading publisher of left-wing material, she wrote about how she, too, felt 'energised' by 7 October. Why? Because this 'defiant' event seemed to expand 'the collective sense of the possible', she said. It made it 'seem as if anyone could be free, as if imperialism, occupation and oppression can and will be overthrown'. In short, it provided a much-needed shot in the arm to depressed Western radicals. It made Marxists like Ms Dean feel a 'sense of the possible' again. It gave their unloved theories about decolonisation and systems of oppression the frisson of real-world violence. Dean admits that Hamas carried out its attack in 'certain knowledge of the devastation that would follow' in Gaza, but she still found it enlivening. Well, what are dead Israelis and Palestinians in comparison with the warm glow of fleeting relevance felt by Western academics who wish it was still 1968?

The university elites' welcoming of the pogrom on the basis that it made them feel 'energised' confirmed their lack of care for Palestinians as well as Israelis. Anyone with even a passing acquaintance with modern geopolitics will have known that Hamas's unprovoked brutalisation of Israel would lead to all-out war in Gaza. To 'certain devastation', as Dean put it. But it seems such a tragic inevitability counted for little in the eyes of those for whom the pogrom became a proxy for real politics. Palestinians and Israelis alike are mere collateral damage in the moral psychodramas of our at-sea cultural elites who crave the thrill of political vitality.

On the streets of the West, too, Hamas apologism ran riot. There were deeply disturbing scenes. On 9 October, before Israel's military response to the pogrom had even properly began, protesters gathered at the Sydney Opera House to burn the Israeli flag and chant: 'Fuck the Jews!' Also on 9 October, thousands of protesters gathered at the Israeli Embassy in London. Why? Israel's invasion of Gaza had not materialised then. There is no escaping the conclusion that they were there not to protest against war but to celebrate a pogrom. As one reporter described it, 'the mood was celebratory, almost jubilant': 'Arabic pop music was blasting, people were linking arms and dancing, while fireworks went off overhead.' 'I support the attack 100 per cent', said one of the attendees. It's a 'blow to the Zionist regime', said another.[28]

This was a pro-pogrom celebration. In London. In 2023. People danced in response to the mass murder of Jews. 'Celebration of Jewish death is implicit in this activism', as one commentator said of the gathering of 'Muslim fundamentalists and affluent socialists' at the Israeli Embassy a mere 48 hours after Hamas's atrocity.[29] The unusualness of that 9 October event, not to mention the horror of it, seems to have been lost to history already. And yet we would surely remember if thousands of Londoners had hit the streets to celebrate *Kristallnacht* – so we should remember that they did it for 7 October.

Then came the marches. London, New York and other cities were rocked, weekend after weekend, by huge demonstrations of pro-Palestinian solidarity that often crossed the line into pro-Hamas sentiment. Placards likened Zionism to Nazism. 'From London to Gaza, we'll have an intifada!', they chanted in Whitehall. The chilling cry, 'Globalise the intifada!', was heard everywhere.

At a London protest at the end of October, the slaughter of Israelis still fresh in Jewish Brits' minds, a group of keffiyeh-wearing Islamists chanted the Arabic war cry: 'Khaybar, Khaybar, oh Jews, the army of Muhammad will return!'[30] That's a reference to the 7th-century Battle of Khaybar that took place in what is now Saudi Arabia, when Muhammad and his henchmen slaughtered Jews, including women and children, for their 'treachery'. These protesters were taunting Jews with tales of their annihilation.

Just weeks after a modern-day army of fanatics had annihilated yet more of them. At some point in the future, when their grandchildren ask what they did following the worst anti-Semitic attack in 80 years, some of London's middle classes are going to have to say: 'I marched with people who made fun of dead Jews.'

It soon became unsurprising to see brazen expressions of support for anti-Jewish militancy. Students at Columbia University organised an event titled 'Resistance 101' at which speakers praised Hamas. One referred to our 'friends and brothers in Hamas [and] Islamic Jihad'. 'There is nothing wrong with being a member of Hamas', said another.[31] In London, protesters chanted lovingly about the 'pro-Palestine' Houthi rebels in Yemen and their campaign of terror against commercial ships in the Red Sea. 'Yemen, Yemen, make us proud / Turn another ship around!', they cried.[32] The flag of the Houthis contains the words 'Death to Israel' and 'A Curse Upon the Jews'.[33] And yet here we had the self-styled anti-racists of the Western left giving moral succour to the anti-Semites of the Houthi set. It was as mad as if the civil-rights movement had cheered the KKK.

Then came possibly the most unsettling element of the West's post-pogrom madness, our Hamas-induced hysteria: the frenzied tearing down of posters showing the Israelis who had been kidnapped on 7 October. Supporters of Israel put up 'KIDNAPPED' posters in cities across Europe and the US. And almost everywhere they were attacked, ripped, graffitied, stomped, binned. Everywhere you looked in London you'd see remnants of the posters, scarred with the jagged claw marks of those who had tried to destroy them. These flapping shreds of paper, with just the eye or mouth of the kidnapped Jew still visible, were a testament to the anti-civilisational delirium that blew up in the West after Hamas's pogrom.

Some posters were defiled with the word 'coloniser' – a clear attempt to rob the hostages of their humanity, to turn them from the victims of violence into the perpetrators of it, from racism's quarry to racism's architects. Horrifyingly, in New York City the likeness of a 12-year-old kidnap victim was smeared with faeces.[34] One of the grimmest images of the post-October moment was found in Finchley Road in London, where the faces of the three-year-old Israeli twins who were kidnapped on 7 October were daubed with Hitler moustaches. Toddlers reimagined as fascists. Jewish children treated as legitimate targets for bigoted invective. It was hard not to hear echoes of past catastrophes. As columnist Dan Hodges wrote of the tarnished twins: 'This is what the Jewish community is facing. Not in 1936. In 2023. Here. In London.'[35]

Anti-Semitism sky-rocketed. How could it not, given the feverish praise for a modern-day pogrom on campuses, on protests, on social media? In the weeks after 7 October, anti-Semitic hate crimes in London rose by 1,350 per cent compared with the same period in 2022. In the US, anti-Semitic attacks rose by 400 per cent. In Germany it was 240 per cent. In France, almost 100 per cent.[36] Jewish shops were attacked, Jewish schools, Jewish people. The word 'Gaza' was scrawled at the entrance to the Wiener Historical Holocaust Library in central London, the world's oldest such library. A teenage Jewish boy was pelted with stones on his way to synagogue in north London. A Berlin synagogue was firebombed. A man set fire to a synagogue in the French city of Rouen. A synagogue in Melbourne was evacuated following the arrival of 'pro-Palestine' activists. Students at the Jewish Free School in London were permitted to remove their blazers while travelling to and from school, lest their school insignia reveal them as Jews to hateful members of society. Young Jews reported hiding their kippahs under baseball caps. It was relentless.

This was more than a spike in hate crime – it was a *continuation of the pogrom*. It was the globalisation of 7 October. It was the internationalisation of the Hamas ideology. It was the furtherance, across borders, of its reactionary edict that the Jewish State is the source of the world's ills, and the Jewish people guilty by association. The West's Hamas sympathisers, the intellectual praisers of its 'energising' pogrom, the disseminators of its one-state propaganda, the witless repeaters of its mantra, 'From the river to the sea, Palestine will be free', and the flagrant anti-Semites who took a torch to synagogues or forced children to disguise their Jewishness – all were amplifiers of the pogrom; all were doing Hamas's bidding; all were the useful 'progressive' idiots of one of the most regressive movements on Earth.

Tortured efforts were made by influencers and the activist class to distinguish their own anti-Israel activism from the anti-Jewish attacks carried out by less civilised members of society. Yet their pleas for moral distinction sounded less convincing with each passing day. It is not unreasonable to see a link between the cultural elites' curiously obsessive hatred for the Jewish State and the re-emergence of hostility towards Jewish people. As Dave Rich has argued in the *Guardian*, it should not surprise us that 'a protest movement that treats the world's only

Jewish State as a transgressor of all moral and human norms' can inflame 'people who do not like Jews'. Rich observes that 'these two phenomena – the anti-Jewish hate crimes and the anti-Israel protests – rise and fall together like clockwork every time'.[37]

The idea that the activist class could single out the Jewish State for special and often unhinged opprobrium, and hint at this Jewish State's malign and disproportionate influence on global affairs, and make excuses for virulently anti-Jewish movements like Hamas and the Houthis, and that this wouldn't potentially have consequences for Jews, seems far-fetched, to say the least. Didn't you people say 'Globalise the intifada'? Well here it is, being globalised. Not only on campuses and outside embassies, but also at synagogues, Jewish schools, Jewish shops, Jewish museums. You would think that an activist class that is hyper-sensitive about 'hate speech', which sees criticism of the Koran as 'Islamophobia' and expressions of biological fact as 'transphobia', might recognise that chanting for a global intifada in the aftermath of an intifada that involved the slaying of a thousand Jews is at the very least a risky thing to do.

What was this fever? What caused the surge of sympathy for a pogrom in sections of respectable society? Why did self-styled anti-fascists cosy up to the fascists of Hamas? Why did anti-racists make excuses for racist violence? Why did feminists whose mantra is 'Believe women' refuse to believe that women were raped on 7 October?[38] How did some of the highest seats of learning in Christendom come to be overrun by apologists for barbarism? Why did posters of children kidnapped by extremists evoke such fury that they were smeared with shit or defaced with Nazi slander? What madness was this?

This is what we need to talk about. It seems to me that the post-October hysteria was the rotten fruit of the West's turn against civilisation. Of our creeping abandonment of reason. Of our trading of the Enlightenment ideals of rational thought and democratic deliberation for the dead end of identity politics and competitive grievance. Having schooled the new generation to be sceptical of the gains of civilisation, we cannot now be surprised that some seem tempted by the lure of barbarism. Having encouraged a culture of self-loathing towards our colonial past, we cannot feign shock that some take pleasure in the vengeful 'anti-colonialism' of a movement like Hamas. Having allowed a cult of 'decolonisation' to flourish in the academy – decolonisation of curricula, of minds, of everything – we have no right to be startled by the noisy worship of 7 October as 'decolonisation in action'. 'What did y'all think decolonisation meant?', asked journalist Najma Sharif. 'Vibes? Papers? Essays?'[39]

And having conspired in the rise of an identitarian worldview that treats whites as oppressors and non-whites as victims, we should not be surprised that this is the only prism through which the young in particular can make sense of the 7 October pogrom and the subsequent war in Gaza. Israel white, Palestine brown. Thus, Israel bad, Palestine good. The 'strange reluctance to see Jews as victims', as Hadley Freeman describes it, has been intensified by these new identitarian ideologies that define entire social and ethnic groups as either 'privileged' or 'oppressed'.[40] The barbarous dearth of sympathy for the dead and raped of Israel is the logical inhumane conclusion to a pseudo-progressive politics that judges people's moral worth by their skin colour, their presumed privilege and their placement on a racial hierarchy fashioned by the unaccountable overlords of Western opinion.

That Israel is not a 'white country', but rather has more Jews of Middle Eastern and North African descent than of European, Ashkenazi descent, makes not the slightest difference to its haters.[41] It has been found guilty of 'whiteness' regardless. And thus it can never be the victim, even when its women are being sexually assaulted, its children kidnapped, its elderly people murdered in their homes. Even fascism can be excused, it seems, if its targets are those who have been damned as privileged by the elites.

The 7 October pogrom raised to the surface of our societies, like scum on water, some of the most disturbing and regressive trends of our time. Clocking these trends, and confronting them, is the great, pressing task of the 21st century.

ENDNOTES

[1] Cornell professor who found Hamas attack 'exhilarating' and 'energizing' now on leave of absence, *New York Post*, 25 October 2023

[2] 'Glory to our martyrs' projected on university campus by pro-Hamas group, *Jewish Chronicle*, 25 October 2023

[3] Palestine speaks for everyone, Verso, 9 April 2024

[4] Israel Gaza: Hamas raped and mutilated women on 7 October, BBC hears, BBC News, 5 December 2023

[5] BLM Chicago goes on posting rampage as it doubles down on its support of Palestine after issuing a sarcastic apology and deleting post using an image of a paraglider similar to the Hamas terrorists, *Daily Mail*, 11 October 2023

[6] Met appeal to find men who wore Hamas-style headbands on march, *Evening Standard*, 14 November 2023

[7] Hunt for Palestine supporters with 'pro-Hamas hang-glider signs', as Suella Braverman vows crackdown, LBC, 15 October 2023

8 Three women convicted of displaying paraglider stickers at London protest, CPS, 13 February 2024

9 More than choosing sides: How Britons are navigating the Israel-Palestine conflict, More in Common, December 2023

10 Majority of Americans 18-24 think Israel should 'be ended and given to Hamas', *New York Post*, 16 December 2023

11 How the paraglider left hurts Palestine, *Compact*, 9 February 2024

12 On October 7, Gaza broke out of prison, Al Jazeera, 14 October 2023

13 Left wing journalist Rivkah Brown apologises and deletes tweet celebrating Hamas attack on Israel saying she wants to 'move forward differently', *Daily Mail*, 11 October 2023

14 Survivors confront their trauma at site of Hamas massacre of music festival, *Times of Israel*, 15 April 2024

15 'Glory to our martyrs' projected onto building at George Washington University, *Times of Israel*, 26 October 2023

16 Rape Culture is a 'Panic Where Paranoia, Censorship, and False Accusations Flourish', *Time*, 15 May 2014

17 Damian Green denies making sexual advances towards young Tory activist, *Guardian*, 1 November 2017

18 'Death to Zionists' chanted in Birmingham campus anti-Semitism row, *Telegraph*, 9 February 2024

19 Columbia Bars Student Protester Who Said 'Zionists Don't Deserve to Live', *New York Times*, 26 April 2024

20 Jewish students face death threats as academics back intifada, *Jewish Chronicle*, 2 November 2023

21 Blindness: October 7 and the left, Hadley Freeman, *Jewish Quarterly*, May 2024

22 Cornell University professor Russell Rickford – who doubled down on saying he was 'exhilarated' by Hamas terrorist attack – now APOLOGIZES and says 'the language I used was reprehensible', *Daily Mail*, 19 October 2023

23 California Islamic Scholar, Adjunct Prof. At UC Irvine, Osman Umarji: Zionists Are Blood-Thirsty Animals; Like 9/11, The Gaza War Is An Attempt By Allah To Waken The Muslims' Spirit; The World Is Losing Confidence In Western Values And Gaining Confidence In Those Of Islam, Memri, 10 November 2023

24 CUNY professor: Israeli Zionists are 'genocidal, racist, arrogant bullies', *College Fix*, 21 October 2023

25 Just another battle or the Palestinian war of liberation?, *Electronic Intifada*, 8 October 2023

26 Albany Law professor ripped for praise of Palestinians 'tearing down the walls of colonialism', News Channel 13, 12 October 2023

27 Jewish students face death threats as academics back intifada, *Jewish Chronicle*, 2 November 2023

[28] 'I support the attack 100%': inside London's Israel embassy protest, *Unherd*, 10 October 2023

[29] Hateful fools will protest at the Israeli embassy – this is why we must let them, *Evening Standard*, 9 October 2023

[30] Racism in the mask of anti-imperialism, *spiked*, 29 October 2023

[31] Columbia suspends students for 'Resistance 101' event at which speakers praised Hamas, *Times of Israel*, 6 April 2024

[32] Protestors chant 'Yemen Yemen, make us proud, turn another ship around' as 200,000 march through London and Met Police move in to make arrests – and Just Stop Oil are there too, *Daily Mail*, 13 January 2024

[33] Houthis show resolve that western strikes will be hard pushed to shake, *Guardian*, 12 January 2024

[34] Visegrad24, X, 14 November 2023

[35] 'Hitler' moustaches drawn on Israeli child hostage poster, *Ham and High*, 26 October 2023

[36] Blindness: October 7 and the left, Hadley Freeman, *Jewish Quarterly*, May 2024

[37] The 7 October Hamas attack opened a space – and antisemitism filled it. British Jews are living with the consequences, *Guardian*, 16 May 2024

[38] MeToo unless you're a Jew, *Unherd*, 17 November 2023

[39] The dangers of 'decolonisation', *spiked*, 28 October 2023

[40] Blindness: October 7 and the left, Hadley Freeman, *Jewish Quarterly*, May 2024

[41] No, Israel isn't a country of privileged and powerful white Europeans, *LA Times*, 20 May 2019

TWO

THE MOST HATED STATE

Has there ever been a state as hated as Israel? No nation provokes the wrath of the West's activist class as much as the Jewish nation. No state's militarism incenses our peaceniks as much as Israel's. No country is as obsessed over, raged against, boycotted and outright feared as much as this tiny nation, the size of Wales, in the Middle East. Thousands of civilians can perish in Syria's civil war, or in Saudi Arabia's Western-backed offensive in Yemen, or in Myanmar, Tigray, Sudan, and not one foot will touch a street in our cities in pained protest. Yet the minute Israel takes action against the terrorists on its borders, the activist class will be buffing their anti-Israel placards, ironing their Palestine flags, fishing their keffiyehs from the closet and hitting the streets to yell: 'GENOCIDE.'

'The hostility heaped on the Middle East's only democratic state, and the only Jewish country on Earth, dwarfs that directed at the cruellest autocracies', writes Jake Wallis Simons.[1] It does. Iran's ruthless repression of the young women and men who rose up against the mandatory hijab law in 2022 barely pricked the consciences of the virtuous of the West. The Uyghurs, so brutalised by the Chinese regime, seem to leave them unmoved. As for the Azerbaijan-Armenia war – who even knows there was a war there? Or that more than 6,000 people were killed in it during

2020? Or even where those countries are? And yet they know everything about Israel, right down to the name of every far-right member of Benjamin Netanyahu's cabinet, so that they can call them Nazis on social media.

Even their own nations' militarism doesn't move or madden the activist class as much as Israel's. Progressives feverishly boycott Israeli wares and culture, taking great care to forcefield their homes and lives from the output of this most unholy of nations. And yet they will happily imbibe American cinema and wear British-made clothes, even though America and Britain's war-making in the Middle East over the past 20 years has caused more deaths than *every Israeli war combined*.[2]

Pre-7 October, around 86,000 Arabs had lost their lives in all the wars fought with Israel since its founding in 1948. The death toll from the post-7 October Israel-Hamas War remains uncertain, but if we accept that it is somewhere in the region of 30,000 (at the time of writing), that would mean around 116,000 Arabs have died in wars involving Israel over the past 76 years. America and Britain's invasion of Iraq caused around 200,000 civilian deaths.[3] Their intervention in Afghanistan caused around 175,000.[4] Our military horrors dwarf Israel's. The righteous of the West who would rather go hungry than eat an orange from the Jewish State, and yet who are more than happy to feast on the offerings of American and British capitalism, have some explaining to do.

The double standards of the West's fashionable haters of Israel became clear during the controversy over the 2024 Eurovision Song Contest. Drag queens and other members of the LGBTQ set extravagantly boycotted Eurovision over Israel's inclusion.

Allowing Eden Golan to perform, when her nation is executing a 'genocide' in Gaza, is an affront to our consciences, they cried. So they closed their gay bars for the night, locked up their drinks cabinets and studiously avoided perusing X for Eurovision updates. And yet these same people will have danced the night away to Britain's naff entries even as we were engaged in that most grim and reckless war in Iraq. Their consciences didn't bother them then. They wanted *douze points* for us, not expulsion. Why Israel's war in Gaza in response to Hamas's unprovoked slaughter of Israelis is a 'genocide' deserving ferocious global rebuke, but Britain's lie-fuelled invasion of Iraq was not, is the question the virtuous cannot answer.

Even in Israel's darkest hour, as it was reeling from Hamas's rampage, they protested against it. As Hadley Freeman notes of the 7 October aftermath, 'There were anti-Israel protests... before Israel had responded'. In London, Sydney and other cities, Israel was being fumed against, insulted, its flag burnt, its Zionist beliefs condemned, before it had fully decided how to react to Hamas's pogrom. It was still counting its dead, comforting its rape victims, breaking the terrible news to the relatives of the 36 children who perished in Hamas's medieval blitz, when the supposedly conscientious of the West were taking to the streets to damn it.[5] This was the salt of Israelophobia rubbed in the wound of the pogrom.

Where was the minute's silence for the hundreds of Jews killed by Hamas? Or for the 39 Thai nationals it slaughtered, making this one of the worst acts of violence against migrant workers of modern times, too?[6] Where were the anti-racists? Hamas is an openly anti-Semitic movement whose founding covenant commits it to a genocidal 'struggle against the Jews'.[7] And whose leading officials were saying as recently as 2021 that Palestinians should purchase 'five-shekel knives' and use them to 'cut off the heads of Jews'.[8] And which had just murdered more Jews in a single day than anyone else had since the Nazis. That seems like something the anti-racists of the West should condemn. And yet their first instinct in the wake of the pogrom was to protest against the victim of that violent orgy of bigotry, not its perpetrators.

Where were the feminists? Hamas is a notoriously misogynistic movement. It had just kidnapped, raped and killed huge numbers of women. Yet feminists, too, certainly those of the intersectional persuasion, were likewise prepping their Palestine flags in the immediate aftermath of 7 October.[9] As for the LGBTQ activists who would later blow up over Israel's inclusion in Eurovision – could they not find one word of condemnation on 7 October for the homophobes of Hamas whose incursion into Israel involved the mass murder of young Israelis of all sexualities at a music festival in the desert? Apparently not. The 'Queers for Palestine' set also responded to the pogrom by protesting against the nation it was inflicted on.

That the activist set's animus for Israel was being cranked up even before Israel had properly responded to Hamas's attack, and long before it launched its full-scale ground invasion of Gaza on 27 October, tells us so much about the voguish loathing for the Jewish nation. It suggests it isn't necessarily what Israel *does* that infuriates its noisy revilers among the Western bourgeoisie, so much as what it *is*. It is less Israel's actions than its existence that antagonises its legion loathers in the West. Their premature fury with the Jewish State, their wrath with a war that hadn't yet started, confirmed that Israel's retaliations are only a part of why they rage against it – more importantly, it's what Israel is seen to represent that excites their fury.

It seems to me that Israel has become a kind of sin-bearer for the woke of the West. A totem of everything they find objectionable in Western society, Western culture and Western history. And they rage against it less for political ends than for personal salvation, as a means of absolving themselves of these supposed sins of modernity. If the hatred for this one state feels irrational, as it so often does, that's because this is not anti-war protest as we once knew it, but something darker, more elemental and entirely regressive.

For some time now, there has been a distinctly visceral strain to anti-Israel activism. The cries against Israel on those recurrent protests feel more guttural than oppositional, more atavistic than logical. You spy it in the language, too. Where other nations fight wars, cause deaths and commit injustices, Israel slaughters, massacres and carries out genocide.[10] We do military interventions, Israel does 'bloodletting'.[11] We cause collateral damage, Israel commits 'murder'. Children, tragically, die in all wars, but Israel actively wages 'war on children' – the words of a high-ranking official at UNICEF.[12] Israel is 'happy to kill children', said a BBC presenter.[13] *Happy*. We're pained when kids die – Israel is pleased.

We do 'friendly fire', those awful accidents that attend every conflict; Israel assassinates. There were so many friendly fire incidents during the NATO intervention in Libya in 2011 that our anti-Gaddafi allies took to painting the roofs of their vehicles bright pink to try to dodge our misaimed missiles.[14] Yet when Israel erroneously fired on aid workers from World Central Kitchen, killing seven, it couldn't possibly have been accidental. No, 'Israel murders aid workers', decreed the *Guardian*'s Owen Jones. 'This is what genocide looks like', he said.[15] We make errors, Israel does genocide.

There is a palpable lurid streak in the media's commentary on Israel's war in Gaza that you don't tend to see for other wars. A writer for the *Nation* describes 'treading through blood' in 'the hell that is now the Gaza Strip' thanks to 'the Jewish State's savagery'.[16] Blood seems to be an obsession of Israel's critics. We hear of the latest 'round of bloodletting'.[17] The 'bloodletting in Gaza' must end, said Khalil Jahshan of the Arab Center in Washington, DC.[18] The Malaysian prime minister, Anwar Ibrahim, went viral among the West's Israel haters when he damned the 'relentless bloodletting' in Gaza.[19]

Online there is a veritable trade in bloody images of the horrors in Gaza. Venture on to social media and you will be 'exposed to a kaleidoscopic view of human suffering without respite', says a writer for the *New Republic*.[20] Anti-Israel activists gleefully share photos of dead children without limbs, even without heads, and cite them as proof of Israel's evil. That similar tragedies occur in all wars – do they think the bodies of the 37 civilians killed by a US airstrike at a wedding in Afghanistan in 2008 were perfectly intact? – makes no difference. All that matters is sourcing 'harrowing pictures' of Palestinians 'covered in blood' in order that others might come to be convinced of Israel's special wickedness.[21]

There it is again: blood. The echoes of older, darker bigotries are hard to ignore. The singling out of the Jewish State as the one nation that fights 'wars on children', the one nation that is 'happy' when children die, coupled with the gory fascination with every drop of blood Israel spills, or rather 'lets', brings to mind yesteryear's irrational dread of Jews. As the BBC reminds us, anti-Semitism in the Middle Ages was frequently fuelled by the 'blood libel' – 'false allegations against Jewish communities of bloodletting'.[22] 'Old blood libels claimed Jews kill Christian children to use their blood for the baking of matzot, the Passover bread', says Israeli historian Gadi Taub: 'Contemporary blood libels claim the IDF is uniquely murderous and deliberately kills Palestinian children to satisfy its bloodlust.'[23]

This vision of Israel as 'uniquely murderous', as the most barbarous of nations, was widespread in the aftermath of 7 October. Owen Jones called Israel's war against Hamas a 'uniquely murderous military onslaught'.[24] Some seem genuinely to believe that the war in Gaza is one of the worst wars ever. It is one of 'the most intense civilian-punishment campaigns in history', says one historian.[25] It is the 'deadliest conflict of the 21st century', claims Oxfam.[26] It is a 'world historical crime', commentators say.[27] Football commentator turned pious tweeter, Gary Lineker, described the war in Gaza as 'the worst thing I've seen in my lifetime'.[28] There's hysteria in this. Literally one of Lineker's own friends[29] – Alastair Campbell, spindoctor for Tony Blair during the Iraq War – helped to bring about a calamity that on every metric was worse than what's happening in Gaza.

Partly, historical illiteracy is at play here. As a professor at the

London School of Economics points out, even a fleeting appraisal of other recent wars – in Syria, Iraq, Sri Lanka, the Democratic Republic of Congo, Sudan, Ethiopia – should make it clear that the 'Israeli-Palestinian conflict is not unique for its civilian destructiveness'.[30] In those conflicts, hundreds of thousands died, dwarfing the toll of the war Hamas started on 7 October. Venture back to before the 21st century and the dangerous idiocy of the idea that Israel's pursuit of Hamas is 'uniquely murderous' becomes even clearer. The Iran-Iraq War of the 1980s, the Cambodian calamity of the 1970s, the Second World War – these were conflicts in which the dead numbered in the millions.[31] Israel's war on the pogromists who murdered its citizens on 7 October is a local clash, albeit a very important one, in comparison with these battles and outrages of recent decades.

Yet there is also something more here than historical ignorance. Something darker. Jake Wallis Simons describes it as a process of 'demonisation', which he says is 'the first characteristic of Israelophobia'.[32] It springs from a feverish 'preoccupation with the evils of the Jewish State', he says, which can condition people to believe, contrary to all the evidence, that Israel really is a 'uniquely murderous' nation.[33] It strikes me that this ceaseless defamation of the Jewish State, the frenzied exaggeration of its 'crimes', the ruthless prioritisation of the pain of its victims over and above the pain experienced by every other human being caught up in war, has nothing whatsoever to do with being anti-war. On the contrary, it is a crusade of vilification against a small foreign state that has more in common with the practices of imperialism itself than it does with the moral principles of imperialism's critics.

Fifteen years ago, the great Jewish novelist, Howard Jacobson, analysed the intolerance and even cruelty of contemporary anti-Israel sentiment. This 'hatred of Israel expressed in our streets, on our campuses, in our newspapers, on our radios and televisions' is the child of bigotry, not progress, he said. It is a 'discriminatory, over-and-above hatred, inexplicable in its hysteria and virulence'. It is 'an unreasoning, deranged and as far as I can see irreversible revulsion that is poisoning everything we are supposed to believe in here – the free exchange of opinions, the clear-headedness of thinkers and teachers, the fine tracery of social interdependence we call community relations, modernity of outlook, tolerance, truth'. When this hatred is at large, he wrote, you can 'taste the toxins on your tongue'.[34]

And its cruellest component? The marshalling of the historical suffering of the Jews to the end of shaming and isolating the modern Jewish State. Why, Jacobson asked, do activists 'call the Israelis Nazis and liken Gaza to the Warsaw Ghetto' when there are any number of 'besieged and battered cities… in however many thousands of years of pitiless warfare' that they could reference instead? Because they want to hurt Jewish people. *That's the aim.* The Holocaust is mentioned 'to wound Jews', he said, 'to punish them with their own grief'.[35]

In the years since Jacobson diagnosed the illiberal, unforgiving nature of anti-Israel activism, things have worsened. The fallout from 7 October made that clear. Virtually every weekend we witnessed that callous urge to 'punish the Jews with their own grief' as protesters against Israel waved placards showing the Star of David mangled with the Nazi swastika or damning Netanyahu as the new Hitler.[36] The tendency of the 'unreasoning' hatred for Israel to harm society itself has been much in evidence, too. London's Jews took to avoiding the city centre when anti-Israel marches were taking place. London risked becoming a 'no-go zone for Jews', said the British government's counter-extremism commissioner.[37]

As for truth, the fabricated claims about Israel's 'unique' levels of barbarism have made short shrift of that. And what is freedom of expression worth if people feel they cannot go into their own city squares with an Israeli flag or a banner saying 'Hamas are terrorists' for fear of assault?[38] The Iranian dissident Niyak Ghorbani was rounded on by the anti-Israel mob and even arrested by the police for holding just such a banner in London – a testament to the dogmatic climate fashioned by the imperious marchers against the world's only Jewish nation.[39] Jacobson had it right – Israelophobia 'poisons everything'.

The anti-Israel elites' claim to be a peace movement has never felt more false. The demonstrations on our streets, the tortured anti-Israel screeds in our newspapers, the 'pro-Palestine' encampments on university campuses – all seem powered more by dreams of destruction than dreams of peace. More by a lofty urge to punish the Jewish State, with violence if necessary, than by a longing to secure a peace deal between Israelis and Palestinians.

Witness the fashion for hollering, 'From the river to the sea, Palestine will be free' – a slogan activists borrowed from Islamists for whom it means the removal of the Jewish State entirely, and thus Jews, from the land between the river Jordan and the Mediterranean Sea.[40] Or listen to the Ivy League Israel-loathers at Columbia University in New York City who denounce Israel as 'the pigs of the Earth'[41] and chant: 'We don't want no two states / We want '48!'[42] That is, before 14 May 1948, a time when the modern state of Israel did not yet exist. They want a world without Israel. They want to lay waste to the national home of the Jews. As the Democratic congressman Ritchie Torres said of that chant that rang out on the manicured lawns of Columbia, 'Turning the clock back to 1948 means wiping Israel off the map.'[43]

What kind of peace movement openly dreams of obliterating a nation? What kind of peace movement deploys the language of imperialism to brand one small country a 'rogue state', a 'pariah state', a 'criminal state'[44], all the better to justify a regime of sanctions, and possibly even military action, against it? We need an 'immediate international intervention' and a 'multilateral combat force' to go and knock together the heads of the Israelis and Palestinians, proposes one observer.[45] Peaceniks for militarism.

A US poll found that 51 per cent of American youths think Israel should be ended and the land given to the Palestinians.[46] A UK poll found that 54 per cent of British 18- to 24-year-olds agreed with the statement, 'the State of Israel should not exist.'[47] Just 21 per cent disagreed. It is now starting to make sense that members of the educated classes would march shoulder to shoulder with radical Islamists hollering for 'jihad!' in the aftermath of 7 October – both have adherents who long to purge the world of the Jewish nation, to liberate humanity from these 'pigs of the Earth.'

The sheer intensity of the loathing for Israel among influencers in the West requires an explanation. Its unreasoning, deranged and discriminatory character, as Jacobson described it, needs analysis. It is completely out of proportion to Israel's size, influence or anything it has ever done. It is utterly out of character with anti-war movements from history. It feels more vengeful than principled, more war-like than anti-war, more regressive than progressive. What is it? What fires it? What informs its acrimony and menace?

What's happened, it seems to me, is that the cultural elites have projected the sins of the world on to Israel. Israel, in their eyes, embodies every wrong of Western civilisation, every crime of modernity, every ill of late-stage capitalism. They charge Israel with it all. It's a white supremacist nation, they say.[48] It's a settler-colonialist regime, they insist.[49] It's guilty of apartheid, imperialism, even genocide. The dragging of Israel to the International Court of Justice to answer charges of genocide in relation to its war against Hamas caused great excitement among the activist class. This is clearly a nation in the grip of 'genocidal mania', activists thundered, and it's a mania that has become 'contagious, spreading far beyond Israel's borders'.[50] In short, Israel is the great corrupter of Earth, the spoiler of men's souls, threatening to ail us all with its disease of inhumanity. They once said that about the Jewish people – now they say it about the Jewish nation.

The Israel haters have come to view this tiny country not only as an impediment to Palestinian statehood, but also as an impediment to peace everywhere – even to the continued existence of the planet. 'Israel's regime of settler-colonialism' is 'responsible for exacerbating the climate and environmental crisis... globally', activists say.[51] Israel's 'carbon capitalism' is bad not only for Palestinians, but for us 'in Europe and Britain' too, we're told.[52] Shorter version: the Jewish nation might just wipe out humanity itself. Perhaps we should eradicate it as a pre-emptive measure, to save ourselves as well as Palestinians.

The anti-Israel set is forever insisting that every injustice in the world flows from or is shaped by the pox on Earth that is Israel. Palestine is a 'climate issue', they say. And a 'queer issue'.[53] And a 'capitalism issue'. It's a 'link in the chain of a wider struggle against the blood-stained, profit-driven system that causes devastation across the world', says a radical writer.[54] 'Palestine speaks for everyone', Western leftists insist. Apparently, the liberation of Palestine is the liberation of *us*: that's 'the radical universal emancipation embodied in the Palestinian cause'.[55] In other words, we're all shackled by Israel. We all languish in its prison of injustice. We are all at risk from its demonic influence. From its contagious genocidal mania, its environmental toxins, its whiteness. You don't need a PhD in the crimes of the mid-20th century to appreciate how dangerous this is, how menacing it is to reason and peace to depict the world's only Jewish nation as being at the centre of a vast global web of wickedness and oppression.

Does it matter that the things they say about Israel are not true? It seems not. It seems not to matter that Israel is not, in fact, a settler-colonialist entity but a post-colonial nation forged from the fires of conflict with Imperial Britain.[56] It seems not to matter that Israel is not a white-supremacist nation, or even a white nation, but a nation where a high percentage of the Jewish population is black or Middle Eastern, and whites are in a minority.[57] It seems not to matter that Israel is nothing like Apartheid-era South Africa but rather is a nation whose Arab population has the right to vote, where Arab parties sit in parliament, and where there are Arab justices on the Supreme Court.[58] And it seems not to matter that, far from being a psychotic outpost of 'carbon capitalism' whose fumes risk poisoning Palestinians and everyone else, Israel contributes a measly 0.005 per cent of global carbon emissions.[59]

No, all that matters is the scapegoating of Israel for the supposed crimes of modernity. The transformation of Israel into the sin-eater of Western culture. The branding of it as the embodiment of every moral violation committed by the white, racist, Islamophobic, transphobic, polluting West, which is how the activist class views this part of the world. Anti-Israel activism is an extension of the anti-Westernism that is now rife in activist circles. Their howls of rage against Israel are howls of rage against Western civilisation itself. Having burdened Israel with all the interconnected transgressions of Western society, they then fume against it in a borderline religious effort to extinguish not only that small state in the Middle East, but also what they have decided it represents: our own moral rot.

This is why anti-Israel sentiment is so unusual. This is why it feels like an 'unreasoning and deranged' revulsion, 'inexplicable in its hysteria'. This is why lies and myths about Israel fall so easily from the mouths of those who hate it. Because this ideology does not belong to the realm of political critique at all. Or to the realms of geopolitical analysis or principled anti-imperialism. No, this is a holy crusade whose true aim is to cast out the Jewish State from the family of nations in the belief that this will cast out the sicknesses of our own societies. It's 'retribution', as Jacobson describes it, where the hope is to 'cancel out all debts of guilt and sorrow'.[60] It is a new damnation of Jews that has the nerve to call itself anti-racism.

ENDNOTES

[1] *Israelophobia: The Newest Version of the Oldest Hatred and What To Do About It,* Jake Wallis Simons, Constable, 2023

[2] *Israelophobia: The Newest Version of the Oldest Hatred and What To Do About It,* Jake Wallis Simons, Constable, 2023

[3] The Iraq war – by the numbers, NBC News, 20 March 2023

[4] Human and budgetary costs to date of the US war in Afghanistan, 2001–2022, Watson Institute, 2022

[5] Israel social security data reveals true picture of Oct 7 deaths, France 24, 15 December 2023

[6] Israel confirms 2 Thai nationals were killed on Oct. 7, bodies being held by Hamas, *Times of Israel*, 17 May 2024

[7] Hamas Covenant, 1988

[8] Hamas official reportedly urges people to 'cut off the heads of Jews', *New York Post*, 12 May 2021

[9] Why can't 'intersectional feminists' condemn Hamas's misogyny?, *spiked*, 21 November 2023

[10] Let's see the 'criticism' of Israel for what it really is, *Independent*, 18 February 2009

[11] The bloodletting in Gaza needs to stop, analyst says, CNBC, 20 November 2023

[12] War on children continues, warns UNICEF deputy chief, UN Palestine, 19 January 2024

[13] 'Israeli forces happy to kill children' jab 'fell below BBC's standards', *Jerusalem Post*, 6 September 2023

[14] Libya rebels paint vehicles bright pink to avoid NATO attacks, Atlantic Council, 8 April 2011

[15] Israel Murders Aid Workers, Destroys Hospital. This Is What Genocide Looks Like., Owen Jones, YouTube, 2 April 2024

[16] Israel's Genocide in Gaza Is a World Historical Crime, *Nation*, 17 April 2024

[17] Israel and Hamas: 'Finger-Pointing Will Get Us Nowhere', *Byline Times*, 12 October 2023

[18] The bloodletting in Gaza needs to stop, analyst says, CNBC, 20 November 2023

[19] The Hypocrites Are Crying Hypocrisy on Gaza and Ukraine, Bloomberg, 15 March 2024

[20] Is the Flood of Graphic Imagery From Gaza Warping Our Perception of War?, *New Republic*, 5 December 2023

[21] The pictures coming out of Gaza are getting worse every day, Sky, 4 December 2023

[22] Israel to fight South Africa's Gaza genocide claim in court, BBC News, 2 January 2024

[23] We Will Defend Ourselves, *Tablet*, 6 November 2023

[24] Who will shine a light on the atrocities in Gaza if all the journalists are wiped out?, *Guardian*, 29 November 2023

[25] Israel's Genocide in Gaza Is a World Historical Crime, *Nation*, 17 April 2024

[26] Israel's war on Gaza live: 'Deadliest conflict in 21st century', says Oxfam, Al Jazeera, 11 January 2024

[27] Israel's Genocide in Gaza Is a World Historical Crime, *Nation*, 17 April 2024

[28] Gary Lineker insists he WON'T stop speaking out on Gaza saying: 'There's a lot of heavy lobbying on people to be quiet but I can't be silent', *Daily Mail*, 11 May 2024

[29] Ex-Tony Blair spinner Alastair Campbell branded 'sick' and 'beyond help' by Tories after he questions how ill Boris Johnson really was when he caught Covid in 2020 and spent three days in intensive care, *Daily Mail*, 22 March 2023

[30] How Unique is the Israel-Palestine Conflict?, LSE Blogs, 8 November 2023

[31] Iran and Iraq remember war that cost more than a million lives, *Guardian*, 23 September 2010

[32] *Israelophobia: The Newest Version of the Oldest Hatred and What To Do About It*, Jake Wallis Simons, Constable, 2023

[33] Who will shine a light on the atrocities in Gaza if all the journalists are wiped out?, *Guardian*, 29 November 2023

[34] Let's see the 'criticism' of Israel for what it really is, *Independent*, 18 February 2009

[35] Let's see the 'criticism' of Israel for what it really is, *Independent*, 18 February 2009

[36] The woke wing of Hamas, *spiked*, 19 February 2024

[37] Adviser warns London a 'no-go zone for Jews every weekend', BBC News, 8 March 2024

[38] Watch: Protester holding 'Hamas Are Terrorists' sign arrested by police, *Telegraph*, 9 March 2024

[39] Judge blocks police ban on 'Hamas is Terrorist' banner protester, *Telegraph*, 13 April 2024

[40] 'From the river to the sea' is a call for genocide, *spiked*, 8 November 2023

[41] 'Pigs of the earth'? Don't you dare call this anti-Zionism, *Australian*, 28 April 2024

[42] A howl of rage against civilisation, *spiked*, 22 April 2024

[43] Ritchie Torres, Instagram, 5 November 2023

[44] It's time to declare Israel a rogue state, Al Jazeera, 25 April 2024

[45] Only U.S.-Led Intervention Can Bring Peace to the Middle East, *Time*, 6 January 2024

[46] Majority of Americans 18-24 think Israel should 'be ended and given to Hamas', *New York Post*, 16 December 2023

[47] Majority of young Britons think Israel should not exist, *Unherd*, 5 June 2024

[48] Settler colonialism, white supremacy, and the "special relationship" between the U.S. and Israel, Jewish Voice for Peace, February 2015

[49] Settler Colonialism, BDS

[50] Israel's genocidal mania is becoming contagious, *National*, 2 February 2024

[51] Palestine is a climate justice issue, Palestine Institute for Public Diplomacy, 31 January 2024

[52] Why the fight for Palestine is a fight for the climate movement, *Socialist Worker*, 19 November 2023

[53] Statement on the War on Palestine, CLAGS, April 2024

[54] Why the fight for Palestine is a fight for the climate movement, *Socialist Worker*, 19 November 2023

[55] Palestine speaks for everyone, Verso, 9 April 2024

[56] *Israelophobia: The Newest Version of the Oldest Hatred and What To Do About It*, Jake Wallis Simons, Constable, 2023

[57] *Israelophobia: The Newest Version of the Oldest Hatred and What To Do About It*, Jake Wallis Simons, Constable, 2023

[58] Israel is not an apartheid state, *spiked*, 26 May 2021

[59] Accelerating emission reduction in Israel: Carbon pricing vs. policy standards, *Science Direct*, January 2023

[60] Let's see the 'criticism' of Israel for what it really is, *Independent*, 18 February 2009

THREE

LYING JEWS

Remember 'Believe women'? It was the slogan *du jour* in the #MeToo years. In 2017, after dozens of women made accusations of sexual assault and rape against movie producer Harvey Weinstein, 'Believe women' became the rallying cry of progressives everywhere. It was on placards on feminist protests. You could get 'Believe women' bumper stickers. There was a full-page ad in the *New York Times*, paid for by the dating app, Bumble, with that simple two-word plea emblazoned on a yellow background. The duty of all good people, we were told, was to take women at their word when they say they've experienced sexual assault.

How things have changed. Since 7 October, since Hamas's campaign of murder and pillage in southern Israel, a new slogan has held sway in activist circles in the West: 'Believe *some* women.' Believe Hollywood actresses who speak out about handsy producers, yes. Believe businesswomen who say they still face harassment in the boardroom, of course. Believe your female friends, naturally. But those women over there? Those women of the Jewish State? Those women with blood-stained pants, bruised faces and broken bodies? Be wary. They might be lying.

The speed with which the liberal mantra 'Believe women' collapsed in the aftermath of Hamas's pogrom was extraordinary. Overnight, we went from a situation where women had to be instantly believed, even when it was just their word against a man's, to a situation where even images of a woman's twisted, burned corpse, naked below the waist, were not seen as sufficient evidence that some form of sexual violation had occurred. This is 'not what you [would] consider conclusive evidence of rape', said the *Guardian*'s Owen Jones upon viewing an image from the pogrom of a stripped, butchered Israeli woman.[1] Yes, maybe her anti-Semitic murderer took off her underwear because he thought his wife back in Gaza would like them.

As soon as reports of sexual violence started to emerge from the ashes of Hamas's pogrom, doubt was cast on them by anti-Israel activists. There was an eruption of 'rape denialism', in the words of Bret Stephens of the *New York Times*.[2] Radical leftists scoffed at 'fabricated atrocity tales'.[3] The *Electronic Intifada* raged against Israel's '"mass rape" propaganda'.[4] This is 'colonial atrocity propaganda', one observer sniffed.[5] A professor at Sydney University denounced reports that Hamas 'carried out mass rape' as a 'hoax'.[6] Palestinian poet Mohammed el-Kurd, beloved of the West's bourgeois radicals, wrote off the rape claims as 'unsubstantiated tales' designed to 'distract from the massive massacres the Israeli army is committing in Gaza'.[7]

Even worse than this noisy denialism of well-known Israel haters was the silence of the feminists. Feminists who have spent the past few years loudly denouncing men like British Tory MP Damian Green for 'fleetingly' touching a woman's knee, and calling on women to think carefully about such profound moral questions as 'who pays for the date', seemingly had nothing to say about the bundling of young, bloodied Jewish women into the backs of trucks by a tooled-up army of misogynists.[8] Far be it from me to mansplain, but if the thought of a hand brushing a knee unsettles you more than the sight of Shani Louk's battered body being spat on and hit with sticks by a mob of violent racists, it's possible you are doing feminism wrong.[9]

The thinness, the sheer moral paucity, of fashionable feminism had rarely been so starkly exposed. Even following the publication of forensic reports on the discovery of female corpses with broken pelvic bones and underwear containing semen stains, the #MeToo set was silent.[10] 'Nothing', wrote Janice Turner in *The Times*, 'from the feminists who at the height of #MeToo threw men to the Twitter hounds for a lecherous pass. Nada from the hashtag activists, open-letter actresses, influencers, podcasters, the period-poverty posse, the menopause matriarchs.'[11]

Even as more 'clear and convincing information' emerged showing that 'cruel, inhuman and degrading treatment' had been visited on the women of southern Israel, there was silence from women's rights activists.[12] Remarkably, not one British charity that focuses on the issue of violence against women condemned Hamas's sexual crimes – apart from Jewish Women's Aid, that is.[13] It took UN Women 57 days just to mention Hamas's violence against women.[14] That's eight weeks. *Two months.* As the world watched Naama Levy, in her blood-stained sweatpants, be brutally spirited into Gaza, and Shani Louk be defiled by the mob, as we heard more and more reports of Hamas's predatory misogyny during its pogrom, there was UN Women, the organisation that styles itself as 'the global champion for gender equality', saying not one, single word.

It was surely one of the greatest betrayals of womankind of modern times.

Some women's groups did speak out – but more in sympathy with Hamas than with the women they brutalised. The head of the sexual-assault centre at the University of Alberta in Canada put her name to an open letter that slammed Canadian politicians for repeating 'the unverified accusation that Palestinians were guilty of sexual violence'.[15] This is a centre whose manifesto says: 'We believe… all individuals who have faced sexual or gender-based violence.'[16] And yet its response to reports of sexual violence by the pogromists of Hamas was scepticism, chin-scratching, a very public expression of doubt. 'Believe *some* women.'

The UK-based radical feminist group, Sisters Uncut, has spent the past few years carrying out direct-action stunts in 'protest against male violence'.[17] Yet in response to reports of male violence on 7 October, these 'sisters' wrung their hands over 'the Islamophobic and racist weaponisation of sexual violence that presents it as an Arab, as opposed to a global, problem'.[18] So perhaps the real victims were poor little Hamas, being bullied by the 'Islamophobes' of the pro-Israel movement.

An entirely new standard of proof, previously unknown in the annals of history, was imposed on those who said there had been sexual violence on 7 October: provide pictorial evidence or we won't believe you. After watching *Bearing Witness*, the 43-minute film compiled by the Israel Defence Forces (IDF) showing Hamas's own GoPro footage of its crimes on 7 October, Owen Jones said: 'If there was rape and sexual violence committed, we don't see that on camera.'[19] Since when did we need to see footage of a rape, a rape snuff movie, essentially, before accepting that a rape had occurred? Others, too, questioned the lack of rape footage in *Bearing Witness*, leading Hadley Freeman to remind them that the IDF expressly said it only included footage that 'preserved the dignity' of the murdered.[20] How 'disgusting', said *Spectator* columnist Bridget Phetasy, that we have gone from saying 'Believe women' to saying 'Rape videos or it didn't happen.'[21]

Nothing better captured the treachery of the feminists than the Garrick Club controversy in the UK in March 2024. In the very month that the United Nations – finally – published a report on the 'clear and convincing information' that sexual violence had occurred in 'multiple locations' in southern Israel on 7 October, what were Britain's starry feminists up to? They were demanding access to a posh, men-only, private members' club in central London. They were fighting for their right to quaff a Cabernet alongside the judges, royals and luvvies of the Garrick. They were hogging the headlines with their demand for access to 'the highest echelons of societal influence.'[22] This vision of wealthy Western feminists storming a luxurious hangout for the privileged as young Israeli women remained chained to radiators in the tunnels of Gaza felt genuinely dystopian. It captured the sinister nature of virtue-signalling, where self-righteous influencers become so obsessed with advertising their own ethical credentials that everything else – even the racist rape of young women – is overshadowed, morally demoted, reduced to a one-column news item, if that.

And what was in that UN report in March 2024 that garnered fewer headlines and less TV chatter than the feminist siege of the opulent Garrick? The report said it was 'convincing' that 'conflict-related sexual violence occurred in multiple locations during the 7 October attacks'. In at least three locations – the Nova music festival, Kibbutz Re'im and on Road 232, the rural highway that was transformed into a 'road of death' during the Hamas pogrom – evidence was discovered for sexual assault and rape.[23] The report points to 'at least two incidents of rape of corpses of women', 'bodies found naked and / or tied, and in one case gagged', and other 'clear' information pertaining to the 'inhuman' treatment of women by the pogromists of 7 October.[24] This was in addition to earlier investigative reports by the BBC and the *New York Times* on the evidence showing that 'Hamas subjected women to horrors before killing them'.[25]

And yet still cynicism reigned among the activist class. Vastly more evidence was found for the violation of Israeli women on 7 October than we had ever seen for the #MeToo cases that became the *cause célèbre* of influencers in recent years. And yet the righteous of the West believed the latter and disbelieved the former. The evidenced sexual debasement of the women of southern Israel evoked their sceptical, questioning side, while unevidenced accusations of sexual assault in Hollywood, the media and the music industry induced instant, uncritical belief. Back then they said to women, 'You are appreciated. You are believed.'[26] Now they say: 'Oh yeah? Where's the footage, then?' It is the most curious and brazen of double standards. And it must not go uninterrogated.

Of course Hamas inflicted inhuman treatment on women during its pogrom. The idea that this anti-Semitic terror group would butcher Jewish children in their bedrooms, throw hand grenades into bomb shelters with families inside and take an 85-year-old grandmother hostage, but draw the line at sexually assaulting young women, is preposterous. It's *that* idea that is fantastical. We know, as Graeme Wood described it in the *Atlantic*, that Hamas's pogrom was an act of 'pure, predatory sadism'.[27] We also know that Hamas is a virulently misogynistic movement. That under its dominion in Gaza women enjoy no legal protection from physical or sexual violence within the family and are 'wildly discriminated against' in the justice system.[28] And we know that sexual violence always attends acts of war. That it has been 'pervasive in conflicts throughout history'.[29] The notion that this mob of misogynistic Jew-haters carrying out one of the worst acts of sadism of modern times suddenly became gentlemen when face to face with the young women they encountered on 7 October is clearly nothing short of a delusional lie.

It wasn't the Israelis who tried to raise awareness about sexual violence on 7 October who were engaged in 'war propaganda' – it was those who pushed this perfidious claim that Hamas committed no act of gender-based inhumanity during its pogrom. That this organisation founded for the express purpose of murdering Jews would never do anything as terrible as rape a Jew. That, unique among the world's radical Islamists, Hamas respects women's dignity, even if it then opts to murder those women. This was the true war propaganda, and it was war propaganda that benefited Hamas, politically, morally and practically.

The rape sceptics of the activist class were essentially doing Hamas's moral bidding. They made themselves its unpaid spin doctors. Hamas furiously denied the accusations of sexual assault, of course, damning them as 'lies and slanders against the Palestinians and their resistance'. And its 'fellow travellers and useful idiots in the West', wrote Bret Stephens, were 'parrot[ting] that denialism in the face of powerful and deeply investigated evidence of widespread rapes'.[30] Remarkably, Stephens said, the self-styled virtuous of the West have pivoted from saying 'Believe women' to 'Believe Hamas'.

This is indeed where we have ended up, in seven short years, between the #MeToo moment and the post-pogrom moment – in a situation where progressives' new slogan, never said out loud, of course, is essentially this: 'Believe fascists.' Believe the fascists who inflicted a pogrom on the Jewish State and disbelieve their victims. Believe the killers of women, not women. How has this happened? How did the West's self-styled anti-fascists end up doing PR for fascists? How did the believers of women become excuse-makers for rapists? Why does #MeToo not include Jews?

To my mind, this is a story of dehumanisation. The holding of the women of the Jewish nation to a different moral standard to women everywhere else is clearly a species of bigotry. The infliction on these women of a higher burden of proof, so that they have to *show* us their rapes before we will believe them, speaks to a stripping away of their humanity. The insistence that they go above and beyond what is expected of the women of other nations before we will accept their version of events is brazenly discriminatory.

Ironically, it has the feel of a neo-colonial crusade, where one foreign nation is singled out for inequitable treatment presumably on the basis that it is morally inferior in some fashion. This one people is to be denied the resources – in this case the moral resources of the benefit of the doubt and belief in women's stories – that other peoples are afforded. The activist class's disbelief of Israeli women is more than just a breach of the principles of #MeToo – it is an imperious indication that the Jewish nation is a lesser nation, an untrustworthy nation, a nation that lies. It marks Israel out as uniquely deceitful among the family of nations.

And the culprit here? The cause of this grossly differential treatment? The reason for this erection of a moral *cordon sanitaire* around the Jewish State so that we might be protected not only from its 'genocidal mania' and carbon fumes, but also from its supposed tendency to lie?[31] It's the politics of identity. It's the new regime of racialism that hides under a banner of progressivism. It's the political class's embrace of an ideology that ruthlessly sorts the world into categories marked 'oppressed' and 'oppressor' and accords or denies moral worth accordingly. The Western cultural elites' ferocious judgement of Israel not only as 'oppressor' but as *the* oppressor is what leads to Israel's unusual, unjust treatment. The brutal exclusion of Jewish women from the moral realm of #MeToo confirms that identity politics has resuscitated racial persecution.

It isn't only the women of Israel who have been disbelieved since 7 October – so also has the entire nation. October denialism goes beyond rape denialism. There is a more sweeping atrocity denialism, too. There is pogrom denialism full stop – a questioning, in sections of the left-wing press and across social media, of whether Hamas really killed and injured as many people as we've been told. It's exaggerated, anti-Israel activists say. It's fabricated, some insist. It was actually Israel that killed most of those people, some claim, in its botched and typically brutish response to the storming of its border by Palestinian 'resistance fighters'.[32]

This conspiracy theory that Israel 'killed its own citizens on 7 October' stems in large part from a *Haaretz* report on 'friendly fire' incidents that may have occurred on that day as the IDF pursued the anti-Semitic militants who were spiriting Israelis across the border.[33] That *Haaretz* has expressly denounced these conspiracy theories – accusing malevolent actors of using the 'disinformation playbook' to 'falsely claim that *Haaretz* corroborated the false theory that the IDF committed mass killings of its own people' – has of course made no difference to the spread of this victim-blaming calumny.[34] As we know from history, conspiracy theories are notoriously impervious to fact and analysis. So just as people in the Middle Ages believed Jews drained the blood of Christian babies, despite not a sliver of proof for such behaviour, so people still believe the evidence-free 'denialist narrative' that it was 'Israel that killed its own civilians on 7 October, not Hamas'.[35]

On and on the denialism goes. In the US, a radical student group said there is no proof that the 'atrocities' Israel talks about 'actually took place'.[36] The Palestinian foreign ministry said Israel was responsible for the deaths at the Nova music festival and that it 'fabricated' the story about Hamas being responsible in order to 'justify [its] war' in Gaza.[37] Perhaps not surprisingly, the Palestinian Center for Policy and Survey Research conducted a poll that found widespread denial among Palestinians that Hamas 'committed atrocities against Israeli civilians'.[38]

What is most striking about all this denialism is that it pertains to one of the best-documented terror atrocities in history. As

Elizabeth Dwoskin of the *Washington Post* noted, 'A crush of evidence from smartphone cameras and GoPros captured Hamas's breach of the border', providing us with a grim vision of 'the most deadly onslaught in [Israel's] history'. And yet still '7 October denialism is spreading'; still we see the emergence of 'a spectrum of falsehoods and misleading narratives that minimise the violence or dispute its origins'.[39] 'It's enough to almost make you feel sorry for Hamas', wrote Hadley Freeman: 'They filmed what they did and made it available and *still* some people refuse to believe it. What's a terrorist gotta do to get some credit around here?'[40]

That even a thoroughly documented act of terror should be so widely disbelieved, so bitterly questioned and chipped away at, confirms that we are confronted by an intense new irrationalism. Or rather, by a new form of an old hysteria – the belief that Jews lie for political advantage. That Jews exaggerate their suffering to fortify their power and influence. That Jews are the masters of manipulation, even able to hoodwink the world into believing they were savagely attacked by Hamas on 7 October. In this way, October denialism precisely mimics older anti-Semitic conspiracy theories. It confirms there are still people out there who want to 'deny that Jews are the victims of atrocity' and to further 'the notion that Jews are secretly behind everything', says Joel Finkelstein of the Network Contagion Research Institute.[41]

October denialism is a modern form of Holocaust denialism. We have witnessed the proliferation, in real time, of the same breed of atrocity-denying delusion that took far longer to spread in the aftermath of the Holocaust. What took decades to emerge following the liberation of the death camps – that is, a bigoted system of cynicism towards the crimes of the Nazis – started to bubble up from the sewer of cranky chatter just days after 7 October. Aided, no doubt, by the viral networks of the World Wide Web, the pre-existing culture of Israelophobia and the coming together of both the hard right and the far left in a shared fear and loathing of the Jewish State, denialism of Hamas's crimes swiftly imprinted itself on the minds of the young in particular.[42]

The core belief of October denialism is that Israel mythmakes in order to add a sheen of legitimacy to its war in Gaza. As Michael A Cohen describes it, the denialists say they are merely 'questioning claims' that are used to '*justify a war* they oppose' (my italics).[43] This is the spirit of Holocaust denialism for the new age. Amy Elman, an American professor of Jewish studies, reminds us that 'the charge that Jews have exaggerated and weaponised their suffering has long been the basis for Holocaust denialism'. In pushing the claim that Israel hawks horror stories about 7 October as 'part of [its] larger nefarious scheme to harm Palestinians', the October denialists are being 'absolutely consistent with Holocaust denialism', says Elman.[44] It should concern us hugely that we have witnessed the staggering back to life of the darkest conspiracy theory of the postwar era – that Jews lie about their own victimisation in order to maintain the disproportionate power they really enjoy. It is further proof of today's crisis of Enlightenment that such sinister speculation, such a wilful dispensing with evidence, such a flagrant disavowal of the recorded truth of the barbarism of 7 October, should have taken hold in sections of our societies.

The true denialism here is the denial of victim status to

the Jews; the denial that 'Jews are the victims of atrocity', as Joel Finkelstein put it.[45] It is the activist class's unwillingness, possibly even its inability, to view Jews as victims that underpins both the outright denialism of the 7 October atrocities and the more mainstream treatment of Israel as the most malign actor in the Middle East. It seems even when Jewish women are being assaulted, and Jewish children murdered, and Jewish pensioners kidnapped, still the title of 'victim' shall not be bestowed on them. In the minds of the modern left, and of the cultural elites more broadly, it simply does not compute that Jews could suffer persecution and thus require our sympathy and solidarity. After all, they're white, right? In fact, they're 'hyper-white'.[46] They enjoy 'white privilege', as the left says, or 'Jewish privilege', as the far right says.[47] They have been sorted into the 'oppressor' category. And how can an oppressor be oppressed? So their suffering is denied, downplayed, ignored, even excused, all to maintain the identitarian order.

It is the inhumanity of identity politics that has sealed the unsympathetic fate of both the Jewish nation and the Jewish people in the 21st century. As Frank Furedi writes, in recent years the 'devotees of identity politics have portrayed Jews as powerful, privileged aggressors, and above all as the oppressors of the Palestinians'. As a result, the Jewish identity has become a 'spoiled identity', 'an identity... that lacks any redeeming moral qualities'.[48] Today, Jews are seen less as the valiant survivors of the greatest crime of the modern era – the Holocaust – than as the enforcers of a new 'holocaust'. Less as the survivors of oppression than as 'beneficiaries of oppression'.[49] Less as an ethnic minority than as white – the *most* white, in fact. Jewishness is arguably 'a form of almost hyper-whiteness', as one US observer says.[50]

Hence, they do not suffer. They cannot suffer. Witness Labour MP Diane Abbott's infamous and clumsy claim that Jews experience prejudice, like red-headed people do, but not racism.[51] Or Whoopi Goldberg's historically illiterate insistence that the Holocaust was 'not about race' because it involved 'two groups of white people'.[52] That is, the Nazis and the Jews: whites, all of them. The recasting of Jews as hyper-white leads even to the denial of the virulently racial intent of the Nazi campaign of extermination, which was expressly an effort by one race, the self-styled 'Aryans', to burn to death another race: the Jews. And witness the frequent branding of the homeland of the Jews as a 'white supremacist' project, where Israelis come to be reimagined, in Daniel Ben-Ami's words, as 'arch colonial oppressors', and the Palestinians as 'the epitome of the oppressed'.[53]

This, then, is the predicament of the Jews. Where once they were seen as insufficiently white, now they are seen as too white. Where once their non-whiteness was held against them, now their supposed hyper-whiteness is used to damn them. Where once they were targeted by white supremacists, now they are branded white supremacists and targeted by the self-styled anti-racists of the activist class. Where once they were killed for their presumed racial inferiority, now the cultural elites turn a blind eye to their killing on the basis of their supposed racial privilege. Where once their suffering was discounted because no one cared about the oppressed, now their suffering is whitewashed, hushed or outright justified because who cares about 'oppressors'?

Then and now, racial ideologies have been a calamity for Jews. If the aftermath of 7 October tells us anything, it is surely that the racial imagination, whether of the fascist variety or the identitarian variety, has no place in a civilised society. No good ever comes from the classification of ethnic groups, the branding of entire peoples as either sympathetic or problematic. It's time we retired all racial thought.

ENDNOTES

[1] We mustn't let the left erase the truth of 7 October, *spiked*, 29 November 2023

[2] The New Rape Denialism, *New York Times*, 5 March 2024

[3] What They Did to Our Women, *London Review of Books*, 9 May 2024

[4] Debunking Israel's "mass rape" propaganda, *Electronic Intifada*, 4 December 2023

[5] Denialism in the Wake of the Oct. 7 Massacre, ADL, 19 December 2023

[6] University of Sydney professor tells first year students that Hamas' mass rapes on October 7 are 'fake news' and a 'hoax', *Daily Mail*, 30 May 2024

[7] Denialism in the Wake of the Oct. 7 Massacre, ADL, 19 December 2023

[8] Damian Green denies making sexual advances towards young Tory activist, *Guardian*, 1 November 2017

[9] Hundreds turn out to mourn Shani Louk at emotional funeral service, *Jewish Chronicle*, 20 May 2024

[10] Their bodies tell their stories. They're not alive to speak for themselves, NBC, 5 December 2023

[11] Why's the MeToo crowd silent on Hamas's rape?, *The Times*, 1 December 2023

[12] The New Rape Denialism, *New York Times*, 5 March 2024

[13] Blindness: October 7 and the left, Hadley Freeman, *Jewish Quarterly*, May 2024

[14] Why did it take 57 DAYS for the UN's women's rights body to condemn Hamas' rape and murder spree? Israel's Ambassador to Britain leads backlash after group 'stayed silent' nearly two months after attacks, *Daily Mail*, 3 December 2023

[15] Canadian sexual assault centre boss sacked after signing letter denying Hamas rape cases, *Jewish Chronicle*, 19 November 2023

[16] Sexual Assault Centre, University of Alberta

[17] Don't just read up on male violence and police brutality. Go out and protest, while you still can, *Pink News*, 15 March 2021

[18] Aren't Palestinians women too?, Sisters Uncut, 2 November 2023

[19] Blindness: October 7 and the left, Hadley Freeman, *Jewish Quarterly*, May 2024

[20] Blindness: October 7 and the left, Hadley Freeman, *Jewish Quarterly*, May 2024

[21] Bridget Phetasy, X, 5 December 2023

[22] Women tried to deliver an open letter to the Garrick Club. True to form – it LOCKED THE DOORS on them, *Canary*, 28 March 2024

[23] Once an artery of thriving southern region, Route 232 transformed into road of death, *Times of Israel*, 13 October 2023

[24] The New Rape Denialism, *New York Times*, 5 March 2024

[25] Israel Gaza: Hamas raped and mutilated women on 7 October, BBC hears, BBC News, 5 December 2023

[26] We should believe women when they raise the red flag, *Herald*, 7 July 2023

[27] A Record of Pure, Predatory Sadism, *Atlantic*, 23 October 2023

[28] Next time Sisters Uncut protest about Gaza, perhaps they could take a look at Hamas's record on women's rights, *Jewish Chronicle*, 1 November 2023

[29] The Devastating Use of Sexual Violence as a Weapon of War, Think Global Health, 1 November 2022

[30] The New Rape Denialism, *New York Times*, 5 March 2024

[31] See Chapter 2

[32] Just another battle or the Palestinian war of liberation?, *Electronic Intifada*, 8 October 2023

[33] New evidence emerges of Israel killing its own civilians, *Electronic Intifada*, 22 February 2024

[34] How Media Outlets Like Haaretz Are Weaponized in the Fake News Wars Over Israel and Hamas, *Haaretz*, 4 December 2023

[35] How Media Outlets Like Haaretz Are Weaponized in the Fake News Wars Over Israel and Hamas, *Haaretz*, 4 December 2023

[36] Denialism in the Wake of the Oct. 7 Massacre, ADL, 19 December 2023

[37] Denialism in the Wake of the Oct. 7 Massacre, ADL, 19 December 2023

[38] Denialism in the Wake of the Oct. 7 Massacre, ADL, 19 December 2023

[39] How the internet is erasing the Oct. 7 Hamas massacre, *Washington Post*, 21 January 2024

[40] Blindness: October 7 and the left, Hadley Freeman, *Jewish Quarterly*, May 2024

[41] How the internet is erasing the Oct. 7 Hamas massacre, *Washington Post*, 21 January 2024

[42] Only 1 in 4 British Muslims believe Hamas carried out rape and murder on October 7, according to survey, *Jewish Chronicle*, 7 April 2024

[43] The Rape Denialists, *Atlantic*, 17 April 2024

[44] The Rape Denialists, *Atlantic*, 17 April 2024

[45] How the internet is erasing the Oct. 7 Hamas massacre, *Washington Post*, 21 January 2024

[46] *Israelophobia: The Newest Version of the Oldest Hatred and What To Do About It*, Jake Wallis Simons, Constable, 2023

[47] Jewish privilege is a myth, *Unherd*, 18 February 2021

[48] The woke scapegoating of the Jews, *spiked*, 12 October 2023

[49] Explaining the left's anti-Semitism denial, Radicalism of Fools, 6 May 2024

[50] *Israelophobia: The Newest Version of the Oldest Hatred and What To Do About It*, Jake Wallis Simons, Constable, 2023

[51] The Diane Abbott row reveals the poison of woke anti-Semitism, *spiked*, 29 May 2024

[52] Whoopi Goldberg suspended from *The View* after saying Holocaust 'isn't about race', *Guardian*, 2 February 2022

[53] Explaining the left's anti-Semitism denial, Radicalism of Fools, 6 May 2024

FOUR

HOLOCAUST ENVY

One of the most striking things in the aftermath of 7 October was the silence of the fascism-spotters. You know these people. They're the centrists and liberals who see fascism everywhere. Who think everything is 'like the 1930s'. The vote for Brexit, Donald Trump, the rise of populist parties in Europe – all of it reminds them of the Nazi years. And yet when the Islamofascists of Hamas stormed the Jewish State and butchered a thousand Jews, suddenly they went quiet. No more Nazi talk. No more trembling warnings of a return to 'the dark days of the 1930s'. No more handwringing over 'new Hitlers'. It seems that to a certain kind of liberal, everything is fascism except fascism.

These are the people who lapped up *Guardian* articles with headlines like 'The reich stuff', exploring the supposed 'comparisons between Donald Trump and Adolf Hitler'. They're the people who will have nodded in vigorous agreement when a spokesperson for Joe Biden slammed Trump for parroting 'the autocratic language of Adolf Hitler'. They're the folk who no doubt permitted themselves a chuckle when it was revealed that Biden staffers refer to Trump as 'Hitler pig' behind closed doors.[1] They're the self-styled 'vigilant' members of respectable society who will have cheered when Biden described Trumpism as a 'semi-fascism' that threatens the 'soul' of the free world.[2]

They're the pro-EU middle classes who fretted over the vote for Brexit, viewing it as a 'return to the 1930s'. They're the broadsheet readers who will have murmured in agreement with headlines saying there are 'terrifying parallels between Brexit and the appeasement of Hitler'. They're the royalty-sceptics who will have found themselves in agreement with princes for once when Charles, then Prince of Wales, said populism has 'deeply disturbing echoes of the dark days of the 1930s'.[3] They're the weekend marchers who will have attended anti-Trump demos at which people waved placards showing Trump with a Hitler tache, and anti-Brexit protests at which speakers issued dire warnings about our descent into Hitlerite mania.

There was a time when you couldn't open a newspaper or peruse social media without seeing some pained liberal hold forth on how populism will drag us back to the death camps. Fascism panic was the fashion of the day. And then it stopped. In the wake of the 7 October pogrom – the worst act of slaughter against the Jews since that period of the mid-20th century these people love talking about – their fascism chatter evaporated. In fact, they started warning people *not* to use Nazi analogies. Not to compare 7 October to the 1930s. Not to engage in the very fascism fretting that had been the bread and butter of their own political commentary for years.

Just two weeks after the pogrom, the *Guardian* published a piece denouncing Israel for 'weaponising the Holocaust' in its response to Hamas's assault. It is an outrage, it argued, that Israeli leaders are likening Hamas to fascist Germany and thus portraying Israel as 'powerless Jews in a struggle against Nazis'.[4] This is the same *Guardian* that had been namedropping the Holocaust for years.

Which ran pieces asking 'Are we living through another 1930s?' after the vote for Brexit.[5] Which published columns saying that, thanks to Trump, 'the world could be heading back to the 1930s'.[6] Yet when Israelis suggested that the slaughter of a thousand Jews by fascistic men with knives, guns and rocket launchers was somewhat reminiscent of the 1930s, the *Guardian* essentially tut-tutted.

It is fine, it seems, to ponder on 'the reich stuff' of Trumpism and Brexit.[7] But it is terrible – 'dangerous', in fact – for the Jewish State to say the Jew-killers who invaded its lands on 7 October echoed the evils of Nazi Germany.[8] Do Guardianistas not think that Hamas has 'the reich stuff'? That this movement whose founding charter promised to 'fight Jews and kill them' is at least a little Hitlerish?[9] What about the pogromist who took a break from his no doubt exhausting barbarism on 7 October to phone home and boast to his parents that he had 'killed 10 [Jews] with my own hands'?[10] Would they call him a 'Hitler pig', as they no doubt enjoy hearing Biden staffers say about Trump?

Other centrist publications that have likewise spent the populist era panicking about the resuscitation of fascism also turned coy in the aftermath of 7 October. A writer for *Time* magazine thundered on the 'danger' of 'using Holocaust analogies right now'. We are witnessing the 'Holocausting' of the 'Israeli psyche', he said, where Israeli leaders are 'using historical trauma to advance their agendas'.[11] He criticised Israel's envoy to the UN for wearing a yellow star while speaking to the Security Council three weeks after the pogrom – this is 'not a proportionate historical comparison', we were told.

Is this the same *Time* that loved comedian Louis CK's

description of Donald Trump so much that it put it in a headline, 'The guy is Hitler'?[12] The same *Time* where a writer warned that Trump in the White House represented a 'new dawn of tyranny' that was not unlike the 'rise of fascism in the 1920s and 1930s'?[13] So had *Time*'s 'psyche' also been 'Holocausted'? Or is it only when the Jewish State uses fascism analogies that we need to reach for the Freudian analysis?

Business Insider also took umbrage at the Israeli envoy's yellow-star stunt at the UN, reporting that he had 'disgraced the memory of the Holocaust' by 'comparing war on Hamas to WW2'.[14] This is the same *Business Insider* that has been churning out Trump / Hitler clickbait for years. Which reported that Trump's rhetoric 'increasingly [mirrors] Nazi talking points'.[15] Which got anti-Trump social media all a flutter by pointing out that the 'Trump cards' his supporters are encouraged to carry in their wallets feature a 'right-facing golden eagle' reminiscent of the Nazi-era *Reichsadler* eagle, which 'also faces right'.[16] Which reported on CNN's comparisons of Trump's 'false-propaganda tactics' to 'Nazi tactics'.[17]

Did that 'disgrace the memory of the Holocaust', too? Did that ceaseless marshalling of the darkest moment in human history to try to land a few blows on the man the coastal elites love to hate, to the extent of madly suggesting a picture of an eagle on some plastic cards might be a sly nod to Nazism, also demean the historical memory of the Holocaust? Or is it only problematic when the nation built by descendants of the Holocaust says that something in the present is reminiscent of the Holocaust?

The centrists' overnight conversion to no longer talking about the Nazis was summed up in the figure of Gary Lineker. This is the

BBC's top sports commentator whose social-media handwringing over the Tories and Brexit made him the moral conscience of Britain's depressed liberals. He caused a storm in early 2023 when he said the then home secretary, Suella Braverman, had used language that was 'not dissimilar to that used by Germany in the 30s'.[18] Braverman had made a speech promising to 'stop the boats' containing illegal immigrants that frequently set sail from France for England. It was this proposal of a policy for better policing at Britain's border that made Lineker feel he had been transported into some kind of fascistic cosplay.

Given his sensitivity to things that are 'not dissimilar' to the 1930s, you might have expected him to have something to say just a few months later in 2023 when Hamas carried out the worst mass murder of Jews since the Nazi era. When young Jews at a music festival were rounded up and put in trucks to be transported to enemy territory. When Jews' homes were set on fire by a marauding mob of men who are members of an organisation whose leaders incite people to buy cheap knives and 'cut off the heads of Jews'.[19] Alas, no. Lineker's social-media feed was curiously politics-free in the aftermath of the pogrom. He promoted his various podcasts and congratulated Tottenham Hotspur for getting to the top of the Premier League, but he seemingly couldn't find the time to comment on a world-historical atrocity that really was 'not dissimilar' to the 1930s.

How do we make sense of this sudden falling out of fashion of Nazi analogies? Why, for years, was it seen as legitimate to dredge up the 1930s in every chat about populism, but now we were being told it is 'dangerous', 'disgraceful' and 'distorting'[20] for Israel and its supporters to say the words 'Hamas' and 'Nazi' in the same breath? Why was it fine for the liberal elites to use the spectre of the Holocaust to underline their furious opposition to Brexit and Trump, but when Israel mentioned the Holocaust following the murder of a thousand of its people, that was a sick exploitation of 'historical trauma'?[21]

It is tempting to see it as just hypocrisy. Just another case of the political class saying one thing and doing another. But there is something else at work in this jealous ringfencing of the right to use Nazi analogies. This arrogant hoarding of Holocaust comparisons for the liberal establishment alone. This reprimanding of the Jewish State for having the temerity to talk about recent Jewish history.

More broadly, it speaks to a sinister separating of the Holocaust from the Jews. To a creeping severance of the memory of that most calamitous event from the lives of the very people who experienced it. The cultural elites' finger-wagging at the Jewish nation for mentioning the Holocaust in its condemnations of Hamas, even as they themselves throw around Nazi analogies like confetti, is fundamentally a calling into question of the Jews' moral ownership of the Holocaust. It essentially says: 'This isn't your historical reference point anymore. It's ours.'

Western liberals' covetous seizing of the right to use Holocaust analogies speaks to a wrenching of the Holocaust from its true context. It speaks to the removal of the Holocaust from its historical specificity, and from the people it was visited on, and its transformation instead into a free-floating symbol of general human wickedness that the privileged of the West can conjure up to add weight to their angst about political life in the 21st century.

It speaks to the *dejudification* of the Holocaust: an unnerving intellectual trend that has profoundly troubling implications for historical memory, truth and freedom itself.

The admonishment of the Jewish State for mentioning the Holocaust following the pogrom of 7 October was swift and severe. 'Stop weaponising the Holocaust', screamed a headline in the *Hill* – at Israel, of course.[22] Members of the activist class even hit the streets to scold Israel for its supposed Holocaust exploitation. Three weeks after the pogrom, members of Jewish Voice for Peace stormed Grand Central Station in New York City with banners saying 'Never Again For Anyone'.[23] Their action was celebrated by observers as an effort to 'disrupt' how 'the Holocaust can be deployed' by Israel to 'rationalise and spin' its war in Gaza. They were cheered for taking a stand against Israel's 'weaponising… of the Holocaust'.[24] So the same activist class whose adherents were noisily likening Israel's war on Hamas to a Hitler-style genocide were also actively 'disrupting' Israel's ability to make any such Nazi comparisons. Holocaust analogies for me, but not for thee.

The chiding of Israel for its Holocaust talk went global following Jonathan Glazer's controversial speech at the Oscars in March 2024. Glazer won the gong for best international film for *The Zone of Interest*. It tells the story of Rudolf Höss, the commandant of the Auschwitz death camp, and his family's idyllic life of horrifying indifference in their stately home next door to the factories of death in which a million Jews were vaporised. In his acceptance speech, Glazer, who was flanked by his fellow Jewish colleagues, said: 'We stand here as men who refute their Jewishness and the Holocaust being hijacked by an occupation which has led to conflict for so many innocent people, whether the victims of 7 October in Israel or the ongoing attack on Gaza.'[25]

Hijacked. That's what Israel does, apparently, to justify occupation and war – it hijacks its people's own past suffering and launders it as a *casus belli*. It milks its own people's pain to make war on Palestinians. Glazer's chastising of Israel was loudly cheered by voices on the left. How great to see a cultural figure 'directly addressing Zionists' who have indeed 'hijacked the Holocaust to justify relentless attacks on civilians', said one left-wing publication.[26] Glazer is right, declared *Haaretz*: 'Jewishness and the Holocaust have been hijacked by the occupation.'[27] He was backed by more than 150 creatives who signed an open letter likewise denouncing Israel for its 'weaponisation of Jewish identity and the memory of the Holocaust' to justify its 'genocide in the making' in Gaza.[28]

Howard Jacobson captured the dark, disquieting nature of these accusations against the Jewish nation. 'Hijack!', he wrote. 'Consider the import of that word. So despicable are the Jews, they will steal from themselves the most hellish events in their history to justify visiting hell on others.' The end result, he said, is the robbing from the Jews 'of any lingering sympathy they might yet enjoy as victims of [the] inhumanity *The Zone of Interest* depicts'. Instead, the Holocaust itself comes to be seen as 'just another gambit in Jewish subterfuge', yet another thing the Jews will exploit for military and political gain.[29]

What was most notable about the post-October explosion of concern for the historical sanctity of the Holocaust was how new it was, what a break it represented from the attitudes of the very recent past. For we live in an era of wilful Holocaust exploitation. Actual 'hijacking' of the Holocaust to make a political point or boost a social-justice campaign has been all the rage for decades. Across the Western world, political leaders, the media elites and leftish activists have summoned up the Holocaust to try to get eyes on their pet causes. And yet those of us who have raised concerns that this diminishes the Holocaust, that comparing everything from trans-sceptical commentary to factory farming with the greatest crime in history threatens to rob that crime of its uniqueness, have often struggled to win an audience.[30] Then, all of a sudden, after Hamas murdered a thousand Jews and the Jewish State said it was reminiscent of Nazism, everyone started agonising over what a grave insult it is to dead Jews to 'hijack' their pain in this way.

It's a shame this respect for the memory of the Jews murdered by the Nazis was so lacking when People for the Ethical Treatment of Animals (PETA) launched its grotesque awareness-raising campaign describing a meat dinner as the 'Holocaust on your plate'.[31] Or when PETA put up posters showing cow carcasses under the title, 'The Final Indignity', as if making beef was comparable to the extermination of six million human beings. Or when trans activists hysterically use terms like 'transgender genocide' to refer to the discrimination trans people allegedly face.[32] Or when the New Statesman emblazoned the words, 'The Next Holocaust', on its front page, positing that Islamophobia in Europe might drag us towards another round of Nazi-style extermination: '[What] we did to Jews we may now do to Muslims.'[33] Or when Muslim News in the UK wondered if Islamophobia is 'leading to another Holocaust'.[34]

Or, for that matter, when wars really were justified through a hijacking of the Holocaust. In the late 1990s and early 2000s, the West's military interventions in Serbia and Iraq were presented to us as just crusades against 'new Nazis'. The Serbs' attacks on Kosovo Albanians 'evoke memories of the Holocaust', we were told.[35] The Serbs are 'NAZIS', said the front pages of the papers, their behaviour containing 'chilling echoes of the Holocaust'.[36] The then German defence minister accused the Serbs of a 'systematic extermination that recalls in a horrible way what was done in the name of Germany' in the Second World War.[37] Both the Gulf War in the early 1990s and the Iraq War of the early 2000s were, in the words of Stanford University humanities professor Russell Berman, 'fought in terms of a metaphor: Saddam as Hitler'.[38] Indeed, George HW Bush said of Saddam: 'We're dealing with Hitler revisited'.[39]

You didn't need to be an apologist for either the ruthless Serb regime of the 1990s or Saddam's unmourned tyranny in Iraq to be troubled by the West's moral appropriation of the horrors of the Holocaust to justify military incursions in those places. As Nazi camp survivor Elie Wiesel said of the Serb question in 1999: 'The Holocaust was conceived to annihilate the last Jew on the planet. Does anyone believe that [Slobodan] Milošević and his accomplices seriously planned to exterminate all the Bosnians, all the Albanians, all the Muslims in the world?'[40]

Words matter. The word 'Holocaust' matters in particular. It refers to a singular event in history, unparalleled in its barbarity, unmatched in its cruelty. Cheapening this word by attaching it to world events that might be very bad indeed, but which are not comparable to the death camps, cheapens the Holocaust itself. It renders it mundane, *ordinary*, just another regrettable thing in our past. 'Just another fuckery in human history', as Extinction Rebellion co-founder Roger Hallam notoriously said of the Holocaust in an interview in 2019.[41] There is no Holocaust on your plate, there was no Holocaust in Iraq, and there is no Holocaust in Gaza. There has only been one Holocaust.

And yet where was the rage against the 'hijacking' of the Holocaust before 7 October? There was some, yes, but not nearly as much as we have seen following the Jewish State's mentioning of the H-word after the pogrom. Indeed, many of the liberals and centrists who've huffed over Israel's alleged Holocaust exploitation were firm supporters of those 'humanitarian' interventions of the 1990s and 2000s that were expressly justified as battles against the New Nazism; which 'weaponised the Holocaust', one might say.

Why the differential stance? Why is it fine, in the liberal mind, for America and Britain to weaponise the Holocaust, but not the nation that was born from the very fires of the Holocaust? Naomi Klein provided a clue in an essay for the *Guardian* in which she celebrated Glazer's reproaching of Israel for its Holocaust-hijacking. We are entering a new intellectual era, she wrote, one in which people are openly asking if the Holocaust should be seen 'exclusively as a Jewish catastrophe, or something more universal'. Where people are demanding 'greater recognition for all the groups targeted for extermination' by the Nazis. Where people are querying whether the Holocaust really was a 'unique rupture in European history' or a 'homecoming of earlier colonial genocides, along with a return of the techniques, logics and bogus race theories they developed and deployed'.[42]

In other words, how special was the Holocaust, really? How

Jewish was it? Isn't it time we treated it as a 'universal' horror, in which everyone suffered, not a specifically Jewish calamity? Klein, in her giddy welcoming of the dismantling of older understandings of the Holocaust, tapped into one of the most regressive intellectual trends of our time: the ideological chipping away at the Jewishness of the Holocaust experience in order that other social groups might lay some claim to the greatest instance of suffering in human history.

We are living in an era of Holocaust envy. The ascendancy of the politics of victimhood has nurtured a palpable hostility towards the idea that the Holocaust was uniquely barbarous. In an era in which victimhood confers moral authority, when the way you secure both social sympathy and state resources is by claiming to suffer 'structural oppression', it simply won't do that the Jews have a singular claim over the gravest instance of victimisation in history. And so their claim on the Holocaust must be questioned, weakened, loosened. What about the other victims of Nazi murder? What about other genocides? Challenging the distinctive nature of the Holocaust, even demoting the Holocaust further down the pecking order of human agony, is the grim inevitable consequence of a cult of competitive grievance in which accruing ever-more tales of pain is the way you move ahead.

As Frank Furedi has noted, in our age of victim politics it is precisely 'the moral authority conferred upon Jews by the Holocaust' that has made Jews 'the focus of resentment among competing identity groups'.[43] Identitarians really do envy Jews their history of torment. Recall when the Muslim Council of Britain (MCB) boycotted Holocaust Memorial Day on the basis that it was 'too narrowly focused on Jewish suffering'. It needs to be more inclusive of 'recent genocides such as that in Rwanda and of Muslims in Srebrenica', the MCB insisted.[44] Or witness the clamour among trans activists to be included among the groups who were targeted by the Nazis for extermination, even though, as one writer notes, there were 'only a handful of trans victims' and, crucially, 'most of these victims were also Jewish or homosexual'.[45] Everyone wants their pound of Holocaust flesh.

The end result of making the Holocaust a 'universal' horror on which all victim groups might gleefully feast is that sometimes the Jews are forgotten entirely. In 2008, Britain's Socialist Workers Party handed out leaflets outside a festival organised by the far-right British National Party. The leaflets reminded attendees of the horrors of the Holocaust in which 'thousands of LGBT people, trade unionists and disabled people were slaughtered'.[46] Spot the omission? *They forgot the Jews.* The SWP chalked it up to an administrative error, but as its rivals in the Alliance for Workers' Liberty pointed out, 'for such a slip to pass unnoticed through writer, typesetter, printer, organisers and distributors, without anyone at any stage picking it up, must say something'.[47]

Indeed it must. What it says is that the reimagining of the Holocaust as a universal catastrophe rather than a Jewish one, a process that Naomi Klein and others gravely mistake for a progressive intellectual endeavour, can lead to the erasure of the Jews. It can nurture new, insidious forms of Holocaust denial. It is not surprising that a poll carried out at the end of 2023 found that 20 per cent of Americans aged 18 to 29 believe the Nazi murder of six million Jews is made up. An additional 30 per cent said they were unsure whether the Holocaust really happened.[48] In 2007, a poll in the UK found that 28 per cent of Britons aged 18 to 29 'don't know' if the Holocaust happened.[49] Some ascribe this ignorance to poor schooling. Perhaps. But it seems unquestionable that the ideological rebranding of the Holocaust as a general horror in which all were victimised is making it more difficult for people to understand the true nature of this industrialised act of anti-Semitic mania. Jealousy of Jewish suffering is the new means through which Jewish suffering comes to be forgotten, even denied.

And now we have the activist class on the streets, forbidding the Jewish State from mentioning the Holocaust while also accusing it of carrying out a new Holocaust in Gaza. It is essential that we appreciate what is taking place here: this is the gloating of the victors in the ideological struggle over the Holocaust. It is the crowing of that section of political society that has succeeded in 'liberating' the Holocaust from the Jews and making it the moral property of others, in particular the Palestinians and their Western supporters. It is the exaltation of an ascendant new class of self-styled victims glorying in their colonisation of the Holocaust for themselves. When they damn Israel for weaponising the Holocaust while simultaneously weaponising it themselves, what they're saying is: 'This is ours now. We own it. We own your history.'

They are 'berating Jews with their own history', as Howard Jacobson describes it. They are 'disinheriting [Jews] of pity'. It is a form of 'retrospective retribution', he says, where the implication, always, is that 'Jewish actions of today prove that Jews had it coming to them yesterday.'[50] Where the Holocaust was a physical effort to dejudify Europe, today's weaponisation of Jewish suffering against the Jews themselves is an intellectual effort to dejudify the Holocaust. To cleanse it of its associations with Jewish extermination in order that it might be wielded as a cudgel against the Jewish nation in the Middle East and used to fortify the claims to victimhood of the non-Jewish activist class in the West. It is something arguably worse than Holocaust denial – it is Holocaust theft.

The moral fallout from the 7 October pogrom shines an unforgiving light on our crisis of Enlightenment values. Objectivity, in this case the objective truth of the Holocaust, is overridden by the subjective needs and desires of the activist class. Historical truth is sacrificed to ideological gain. Reason and reality are trampled in the rush of identity groups to consolidate their victim status. And our right to remember what really happened in the past is interfered with by ideologues who manipulate the events of history to suit their political agendas in the present. Such Orwellian meddling with the truth of the Holocaust is an insult not only to the victims of that calamity, but also to the freedom of living people today. 'The struggle of man against power is the struggle of memory against forgetting', Milan Kundera said.[51] Let remembering the Holocaust be our small rebellion against the new anti-Semitism.

ENDNOTES

[1] Some Biden aides refer to Trump as 'Hitler Pig', report says, *Independent*, 18 April 2024

[2] Biden decries Republican loyalty to Trump as 'semi-fascism', *Guardian*, 26 August 2022

[3] Prince Charles warns of return to the 'dark days of the 1930s' in Thought For The Day message, *Telegraph*, 26 December 2016

[4] Israel must stop weaponising the Holocaust, *Guardian*, 24 October 2023

[5] Are we living through another 1930s?, *Guardian*, 1 August 2016

[6] Inspired by Trump, the world could be heading back to the 1930s, *Guardian*, 22 June 2018

[7] Are we living through another 1930s?, *Guardian*, 1 August 2016

[8] Israel must stop weaponising the Holocaust, *Guardian*, 24 October 2023

[9] Hamas Covenant, 1988

[10] No one can deny Hamas' aim is to kill Jews – it fully admits it, FDD, 8 November 2023

[11] The Real Danger of Using Holocaust Analogies Right Now, *Time*, 16 November 2023

[12] Louis C.K. on Donald Trump: 'The Guy Is Hitler', *Time*, 5 March 2016

[13] Donald Trump and the New Dawn of Tyranny, *Time*, 3 March 2017

[14] Israeli official disgraced the memory of the Holocaust by comparing war on Hamas to WWII, memorial museum says, *Business Insider*, 31 October 2023

[15] Trump's rhetoric is increasingly mirroring Nazi talking points, and nobody is paying attention, an expert on extremism warns, *Business Insider*, 31 December 2023

[16] Donald Trump wants his supporters to carry a plastic card that critics say looks remarkably similar to Nazi insignia, *Business Insider*, 7 August 2021

[17] Donald Trump, who called mob that included neo-Nazis 'very fine people,' now hits CNN over comparing him to Hitler and Goebbels, *Business Insider*, 29 July 2022

[18] BBC 'speaking frankly' with Gary Lineker over tweet comparing UK asylum policy to 1930s Germany, BBC News, 8 March 2023

[19] Hamas official reportedly urges people to 'cut off the heads of Jews', *New York Post*, 12 May 2021

[20] Israel must stop weaponising the Holocaust, *Guardian*, 24 October 2023

[21] The Real Danger of Using Holocaust Analogies Right Now, *Time*, 16 November 2023

[22] Stop weaponizing the Holocaust, *Hill*, 4 November 2023

[23] "Not in Our Name": 400 Arrested at Jewish-Led Sit-in at NYC's Grand Central Demanding Gaza Ceasefire, Democracy Now!, 30 October 2023

[24] Stop weaponizing the Holocaust, *Hill*, 4 November 2023

[25] *Zone of Interest* director Jonathan Glazer makes Gaza statement in Oscars speech, BBC News, 11 March 2024

[26] Filmmaker Jonathan Glazer Speaks Out Against Israel's Hijacking of Holocaust to Justify Gaza War, *Common Dreams*, 11 March 2024

[27] Jonathan Glazer Was Right: Jewishness and the Holocaust Have Been Hijacked by the Occupation, *Haaretz*, 13 March 2024

[28] Joaquin Phoenix and Joel Coen sign open letter in support of Glazer's Oscar speech, *Guardian*, 5 April 2024

[29] Who dares to 'hijack' the Holocaust?, *New Statesman*, 12 March 2024

30 How 'Holocaust relativists' on both left and right use the greatest crime in history for political ends, *Spectator*, 21 January 2006

31 Using the 'Holocaust' Metaphor, Society of Professional Journalists

32 Don't believe the activists' hype: There is no 'trans genocide', *New York Post*, 28 April 2023

33 Europe's Persecuted Muslims?, *Commentary*, April 2007

34 Europe's Persecuted Muslims?, *Commentary*, April 2007

35 How 'Holocaust relativists' on both left and right use the greatest crime in history for political ends, *Spectator*, 21 January 2006

36 How 'Holocaust relativists' on both left and right use the greatest crime in history for political ends, *Spectator*, 21 January 2006

37 *Degraded Capability: The Media and the Kosovo Crisis*, Philip Hammond and Edward Herman (eds), Pluto Press 2000

38 *Anti-Americanism in Europe: A Cultural Problem*, Russell Berman, Hoover Institution Press, 2004

39 The Long Road to War, PBS, 2003

40 The Question Of Genocide, *Newsweek*, 11 April, 1999

41 Extinction Rebellion: Co-founder apologises for Holocaust remarks, BBC News, 21 November 2019

42 The *Zone of Interest* is about the danger of ignoring atrocities – including in Gaza, *Guardian*, 14 March 2024

43 The woke scapegoating of the Jews, *spiked*, 12 October 2023

44 Muslim Council ends Holocaust Memorial Day boycott, *Guardian*, 3 December 2007

45 No, JK Rowling is not a Holocaust denier, *spiked*, 21 March 2024

46 Shoah leaflet refers to gays but not Jews, *Jewish Chronicle*, 22 August 2008

47 Has the SWP Discovered a 'Jew-Free' Holocaust?, *Workers' Liberty*, 19 August 2008

48 One in five young Americans believes the Holocaust is a myth, poll finds, *Telegraph*, 9 December 2023

49 UK poll reveals striking ignorance of Holocaust, Reuters, 9 August 2007

50 Let's see the 'criticism' of Israel for what it really is, *Independent*, 18 February 2009

51 *The Book of Laughter and Forgetting*, Milan Kundera, Faber and Faber, 1978

FIVE

THE UNHOLIEST ALLIANCE

Imagine if a fascist group overseas massacred hundreds of people and it was discovered that there are people in Britain who had called the fascists their 'friends'. Imagine if in the wake of their carnival of racist killing it came to light that commentators in the UK had lovingly referred to them as 'uncompromising and shrewd' freedom fighters. Imagine if we found out, as the victims of the fascist attack were still counting their dead and tending to their injured, that there are academics in the West who had praised the fascists as 'progressive' and activists who had lauded their 'democratic' credentials. We would be shocked, right? We would want to know, surely, what had gone wrong in our societies when so many of our influencers could sing the praises of a movement capable of such horrors.

Well, we don't need to imagine. All of the above is true of Hamas's pogrom of 7 October. Jeremy Corbyn, a former leader of the UK Labour Party, a man who might have been prime minister, once referred to Hamas as his 'friends'.[1] Novara Media, the left media outlet beloved of Britain's well-heeled radical millennials, once published a gushing profile of Mohammed Deif, the then head of the Al-Qassam Brigades, the military wing of Hamas. Deif is suspected of masterminding the 7 October atrocity from his hideout in Gaza.[2] He 'embodies the uncompromising and shrewd "freedom fighter" figure', gushed Novara in 2014. He enjoys 'wide popularity' among Palestinians, it fawned, on account of the 'innovative skills' he has deployed to great effect to bring about an 'impressive evolution' of the Palestinian 'resistance'. And he later deployed those 'skills' to organise the largest slaughter of Jews since the Holocaust.

It was Judith Butler, America's celebrated gender philosopher, who cheered Hamas as 'progressive'. In 2006, she waxed lyrical about 'Hamas [and] Hezbollah' being 'social movements that are progressive, that are on the left, that are part of a global left'.[3] Either Hamas changed a great deal in the intervening 17 years, between Butler's effusive praise and its butchery of a thousand Jews, or the word 'progressive' doesn't mean what we thought it did.

It was the radical British leftist, Lindsey German, who pledged her support for Hamas's supposed democratic streak. German was a founder of the Stop the War Coalition, the leftist group that organised the big marches against the Iraq War in the 2000s. At a Stop the War conference in 2006, she said of Hamas and Hezbollah: 'They want democracy. Democracy in the Middle East is Hamas, [it is] Hezbollah.'[4] One is forced to wonder what is democratic about invading a neighbouring nation and murdering, maiming and raping more than a thousand of its people.

As the reports came in on that day of infamy in October 2023 about the extent of Hamas's killing, about the sheer cruelty of its racist mission, I found myself thinking: there are people in Britain who have expressed support for this group. There are people here who have garlanded those killers with praise. There are commentators who have heaped admiration on them for their skill and flair. To me, it was as shocking as if we had discovered in the wake of 9/11 that there were influencers among us who had been eulogising al-Qaeda and cheering Osama bin Laden as a smart, creative freedom fighter.

Where was all the Hamas praise coming from? The left. From the radical wing of the Labour Party, the anti-war movement, and the new 'woke' left as embodied by the media-savvy socialists at Novara. A left that poses as anti-war had been praising a warmongering terror outfit. A left that claims to be anti-racist had gushed over brazen racists whose founding charter states that 'our struggle against the Jews is very great and very serious'.[5] Self-styled anti-fascists had become 'friends' with fascists.

This perverse political marriage between secular leftists and the religious extremists of radical Islam must be confronted. This Islamo-left, as some refer to it, is the unholiest of alliances. How did we end up in a situation where the leader of Her Majesty's Opposition was friends with people who would go on to commit one of the worst crimes against humanity of the modern era?

Jeremy Corbyn typifies the Islamo-left. For years, he has been rubbing shoulders with extremists linked to murderous movements. It was in 2009, when he was a Labour backbencher, that he referred to Hamas as his friends. He was hosting a meeting on the Middle East in parliament, to which he invited Hamas and Hezbollah. It is 'my pleasure and my honour' to invite '[our] friends from Hamas to come and speak', he said. '*My honour.*' The love-in didn't end there. He hailed Hamas as 'an organisation that is dedicated towards the good of the Palestinian people and bringing about long-term peace and social justice' in the Middle East.[6]

Social justice? Where's the social justice in Hamas's treatment of gay people? Homosexual relations are illegal under Hamas's unforgiving dominion in Gaza.[7] Gay people face persecution and torture. In 2021, the Williams Institute at the University of California, Los Angeles conducted a survey of 175 nations and their acceptance of gay and gender non-conforming people. Palestine, covering both Gaza and the West Bank, was at No130. Behind Yemen, Saudi Arabia and the Democratic Republic of Congo.[8] In 2010, just a year after Corbyn exalted Hamas for its devotion to social justice, leading Hamas strategist Mahmoud al-Zahar told Reuters: 'You [in the West] do not live like human beings. You do not even live like animals. You accept homosexuality.'[9] So gay people are lower than beasts. Corbyn was 'friends' with homophobes.

Where's the 'social justice' in Hamas's treatment of women? Under Hamas's iron fist of Islamism, women in Gaza face 'widespread discrimination in the economic and social sectors'. A study a few years ago found that Gazan women's participation in the labour force is among the lowest in the world – only 22 per cent of women there work, in comparison with a global average of 50 per cent.[10] There is no law in Gaza prohibiting violence against women in the home, including sexual violence.[11] Thanks to Corbyn's 'friends', men in Gaza can do pretty much anything they want to women behind closed doors.

Then there's Hamas's tyrannical treatment of opposition groups. In the same year Corbyn cheered Hamas for its love of social justice, Hamas was torturing and murdering its critics. A Human Rights Watch report published in April 2009 documented

Hamas's use of savage violence against members of Fatah, the political party mainly based in the West Bank but with supporters in Gaza, too. It condemned Hamas's 'widespread practice of maiming people by shooting them in the legs', its 'abductions and severe beatings' of its opponents, and its 'extrajudicial executions' of those 'accused of collaborating with Israel'.[12]

In falsely lauding these trigger-happy extremists as purveyors of social justice, Corbyn was essentially providing moral cover for tyranny. This self-styled feminist ally, supporter of gay rights and devotee of fairness was chumming around with a violently misogynistic and homophobic movement that maims and slays its rivals. And his congeniality with Hamas continued. In 2012, three years after his 'friends' speech, he attended a conference on Palestinian affairs in Doha in Qatar alongside leading Hamas figures. They included the then head of Hamas, Khaled Mashaal, and a former top bruiser in Hamas's military wing, Husam Badran.[13] Badran oversaw some of the most obscene attacks of the Second Intifada, including the bombing of Sbarro Pizza in Jerusalem in 2001, which killed 15, and the bombing of the Dolphinarium Discotheque in Tel Aviv, also in 2001, in which 21 souls, mostly teenagers, were extinguished.

It can feel difficult to grasp the gravity of this. The man who won 40 per cent of the vote in the 2017 General Election, who nearly got the keys to Downing Street, had been mingling with Jew-killers just five years earlier. Hamas was founded in 1987 with the aim of obliterating the Jewish State. In 2011, a year before Corbyn hung out with Hamas in Doha, the Hamas cleric and member of the Palestinian parliament, Yunis Al Astal, reiterated his movement's commitment to erasing the Jews from the Middle East. Palestinians, he said, will 'have the honour of annihilating the evil of this gang'.[14] Hamas's military operatives, like Husam Badran, had made good on this promise of Jew murder by massacring hundreds of Jews during the Second Intifada. And yet there was Corbyn at a conference with Badran and other associates of this movement that hates and kills Jews. It was as scandalous as if a Tory MP had cosied up to an army of white supremacists that had murdered hundreds of 'evil' black people.

Corbyn's 'friendliness' with extremists seemed neverending. During a visit to Tunis in 2014, he was seen laying a wreath near the graves of the Black September terrorists – the Palestinian militants responsible for massacring 11 Israeli coaches and athletes at the Munich Olympics in 1972.[15] In 2012, he heaped praise on the extremist preacher, Sheikh Raed Salah, a fundraiser for Hamas and hawker of anti-Semitic crank theories about who was really behind 9/11. After the UK government made moves to deport the Sheikh, Corbyn protested, hailing him as an 'honoured citizen' who 'represents his people extremely well'. He offered to give the Sheikh 'tea on the terrace' in parliament, saying 'you deserve it'.[16] Corbyn also worked for Press TV, the Iranian theocracy's state TV network, between 2009 and 2012. This is the network that was banned in Britain for its alleged part in filming the torture of an Iranian journalist.[17] Maybe that persecution of a dissident was 'social justice', too.

Other British leftists have also made common cause with the feudal theocracy of radical Islam. In 2002, in the run-up to the war in Iraq, the left-wing Stop the War Coalition that Corbyn helped to set up struck up an alliance with the Muslim Association of Britain (MAB). Stop the War, founded in 2001 after 9/11, had been dominated by the Socialist Workers Party and the Communist Party of Britain. Then it decided to embrace MAB, a lobby group founded by activists from the Muslim Brotherhood, the extremist Egyptian movement that gave birth to Hamas, among others.[18] One of MAB's directors, Anas Altikriti, has close links with Hamas's military commanders and has gushed over Hamas.[19] One of its founders, Muhammad Sawalha, was an actual leader of Hamas's military wing in the West Bank in the 1980s.[20] A left movement supposedly devoted to ending war was linking arms with the associates of a movement devoted to waging war, in particular on Jews.

It was Stop the War's Lindsey German who praised Hamas's supposed devotion to 'democracy in the Middle East'. Other Stop the War leaders ventured to Beirut in 2006 to attend a conference organised by the Centre for Strategic Studies of the Lebanon-based movement, Hezbollah – another violently Israelophobic outfit that dreams of liquidating the Middle East of its Jews. Hassan Nasrallah, the secretary-general of Hezbollah, has stated his wicked aim of 'finish[ing] off the entire cancerous Zionist project'. Hezbollah spokesman Hassan Ezzeddin has said that when his 'army of god' finally conquers the Jewish State, the Jews who survive 'can go back to Germany, or wherever they came from'.[21]

In short, Hezbollah has sworn itself to the forced, violent repatriation of Israel's Jews on the basis that they are a cancerous presence in the Middle East – an explicitly racist, genocidal dream. And yet in 2006 we saw the supposed anti-racists of Britain's Stop the War movement happily attend a Hezbollah-linked conference. Most of these people were members of the Socialist Workers Party, a party that rages against the Tories' 'racist' immigration policies and which noisily damns the late Tory MP Enoch Powell and his infamous 'rivers of blood' speech as horrific examples of British intolerance. Yet they were content to rub shoulders with the associates of a movement whose genocidal ambitions make Powell look like a political pussycat in comparison.

That the Islamo-left will associate with non-white people who hold views that it would angrily brand as racist, bigoted and outright unacceptable if they were expressed by white people is telling. This is a left that furiously cancels hard-right activists in the UK, yet it is content to mix with the hard-right Jew-killers of Hamas and Hezbollah. The SWP is devoted to the censorious campus policy of No Platform, whereby the far right, or just anyone judged to be insufficiently politically correct on matters of race, sex and gender, can be denied the right to speak. Yet it is happy to listen to the outpourings of a movement that dreams of waging apocalyptic racial war on the 'cancerous' Jews. The modern left itches to ban women who question the ideology of transgenderism and ex-Muslims who slam their former religion for its sexist attitudes and backward beliefs.[22] It damns the former as 'transphobes' and the latter as 'Islamophobes'. And yet it will gleefully make connections with movements that murder homosexuals, brutalise women, kneecap critics and vaporise young Jews in discotheques. Those people aren't 'phobes', apparently – they're 'friends'.

This striking double standard, this burning contempt for

white bigots combined with a lenient and even friendly attitude towards far worse non-white bigots, speaks to the neo-racism of identity politics. Under the identitarian ideology that the post-class left has feverishly embraced, whites are 'oppressors' and non-whites are 'oppressed'. And thus whites can be criticised, they must be, in fact, every time they give voice to views the left disapproves of. But non-whites must never be criticised. Even when they're likening gays to beasts or Jews to cancer or forcing women to cover their sinful hair and sinful faces with veils and cloaks. To raise objections to these beliefs and practices would only compound the oppression of the oppressed, apparently, and so a blind eye is turned. Such patrician acquiescence to the regressive thinking of Islamists, such silent acceptance of their homophobia, misogyny and anti-Semitisim, is its own form of bigotry. To judge non-whites by a lower moral standard than the one you use for whites is the very definition of racism.

This 'blind eye' policy towards the reactionary hatreds of radical Islam is an essential component of the Islamo-left. As the writer Alexander von Sternberg says, it is remarkable 'how much brutality and bigotry the Western left is willing to excuse in the service of... "decolonisation".'[23] The left's 'blindness' to the backwardness and at times outright depravity of radical Islam confirms that it prizes landing a few blows on 'the West' more highly than it does the equal rights and cultural security of women, gay people and Jews. The left has effectively sacrificed those older ideals of sexual equality and social fairness at the altar of its feverish anti-Westernism, of its obsessive West-bashing that it dresses up as anti-imperialism.[24]

This requirement to be 'blind', at times, to the bigotry of Islamists was spelled out in *The Prophet and the Proletariat,* the 1994 pamphlet by Chris Harman, the then editor of *Socialist Worker.* It is the closest thing we have to a manifesto of the Islamo-left. Harman admits that Islamism at times has the whiff of fascism to it, what with its murderous intolerance towards certain minority groups and its less than enlightened views on women and gay people. And yet there is a glimmer of promise in the Islamist project, he proposed. This is a movement that stands up to 'imperialism's political domination'. It has 'played a key role in the armed struggle against Israel'. It has a 'feeling of revolt', he concluded, that might on occasion be 'tapped for progressive purposes'.[25]

Harman's balancing of the downsides of radical Islam with its supposed upsides gave rise to a willingness in some quarters to overlook Islamism's homicidal bigotries entirely because of that 'feeling of revolt' it promised. Because it might just provide listless leftists in the West with a fleeting moral rush. Why obsess too much over the fascist bent of Islamism when this exotic, rowdy movement could potentially make armchair radicals feel alive for once? Why concern yourself with Islamism's hatred for Jews, women and gay people given that Islamists also hate 'imperialism's political domination', like we do?

It was the historical disarray of the left in the 1990s, its political and moral discombobulation, that tempted it into the pseudo-revolutionary arms of violent Islamists. Still smarting from the withering of class politics at home, and from the collapse of Communism around the world, the left was on the lookout for new constituencies, new crusades, for some semblance of purpose.

And it found it in the apocalyptic violence of radical Islam, a thing that felt real, forceful, like a genuine menace to 'imperialism's political domination'.[26] That the Islamists harboured their own dreams of domination, whether the violent excision of the Jews from their homeland or the slaughter of people in the irreligious West, was immaterial. All that mattered was that Islamists appeared to add the weight of physical force, of violent drama, to the left's own anti-Westernism. They gave an injection of 'revolt' to leftists who were desperate for some momentum in the post-Cold War era. Islamists became the left's new 'revolutionary subject'. It was suicidal opportunism.

Over time, even Chris Harman's acknowledgement of the fascist streak in radical Islam was lost to history. His proposal of a cautious, occasional alliance between the left and Islamism was superseded by outright bed-hopping between these ill-suited movements. Soon Corbyn was calling the Jew-killers of Hamas and Hezbollah his friends. Soon Harman's old comrades in the SWP were flying to Lebanon to hang out with a movement that had promised to drive the Jewish cancer from Israel 'back to Germany'.

Soon there were 'anti-war' rallies in Trafalgar Square featuring Islamist speakers telling a cheering crowd of radicalised leftists and radicalised Muslims that 'if they deny you life, explode in their faces! There will be jihad, jihad and jihad!' Soon there were Stop the War protests at which banners were unfurled saying, 'We are all Hezbollah now'.[27] Soon radical leftists were even cheering the 'Iraqi insurgency', a sinister movement of Sunni extremists and al-Qaeda affiliates that was engaged in sectarian warfare, planting bombs in marketplaces and blowing up groups of children.[28]

Soon Islamic preachers were being 'allowed to conduct prayers and invoke Allah' on the stage at anti-war rallies.[29] Soon the Stop the War Coalition was even allowing the segregation of the sexes at some of its meetings, in order not to offend its new Islamist allies.[30] And when Stop the War was pressed on this, when it was interrogated by its critics on its craven submission to an Islamist requirement, one of its leaders described women's rights and gay rights as a 'shibboleth' that must not be allowed to 'get in the way of unity with Muslim groups' against imperialism.[31] How quickly the rights of half the population and of historically oppressed groups can become 'outmoded' and 'not important' – to give 'shibboleth' its meaning – when alliances with extremists are made.

And soon leftists were cheering the Hamas incursion. 'Rejoice as Palestinian resistance humiliates racist Israel', said the headline in *Socialist Worker* after the 7 October pogrom.[32] *Rejoice.* This was published on 9 October, when the world knew what Hamas had done. When we were aware of its carnage against citizens. And soon there were people on 'pro-Palestine' marches wearing images of paragliders in tribute to the fascists who paraglided into Israel on 7 October to murder Jewish women and children.[33] Soon leftists were chanting favourably about the Houthis, the Yemeni movement whose slogan is 'A Curse Upon the Jews' and 'Death to Israel'.[34] Soon students in the US were being told that there is 'nothing wrong with being a fighter in Hamas'.[35] Soon leftist agitators were dreaming of erasing 'the pigs of the Earth' from the Middle East and going back to '48' – 1948, that is, when Israel, in its modern form, did not exist.

They really are 'all Hezbollah now'. They really do share in

Hezbollah's dream of 'finish[ing] off the entire cancerous Zionist project'.[36] 'Islamo-left' is a moot phrase, for vast swathes of the left are of that persuasion now. The sight, in the aftermath of 7 October, of genteel liberals marching alongside pro-Houthi leftists and radical Islamists demanding more jihad (that is, more pogroms) against the Jewish nation was confirmation, surely, that the suicidal alliance of Islamism and leftism is now a wholly mainstream thing. A yearning for holy war on Israel and everything it is seen to represent – Western ideals, post-colonial confidence, Jewish pride – is what unites both the Islamic extremist and the genderfluid leftist in this strange, unstable century.

The Islamo-left alliance began with the left holding its nose, yet it has ended with the left merrily breathing in the fumes of the Islamist ideology. It started with Harman reminding leftists that some Islamists are fascists, yet it has ended with leftists glorying in their friendships with these fascists, and in the ideas of these fascists, and even in the violence of these fascists. It started as a sad, pathetic search for a 'feeling of revolt' in the post-Communist era, yet it has ended in public displays of celebration over Hamas's 'revolt' against the Jews. It's a lesson as old as time: make a deal with the devil and the devil will always win. A left that thought it could make just the occasional alliance with fascism now finds itself at the service of fascism, dutifully doing Hamas's and Hezbollah's bidding on the streets of our cities.

Nothing better illustrates the absorption of the left into the moral universe of Islamism than the fact that the left won't even permit criticism of Islamism anymore. When this deathly union first emerged in the 1990s there was some discussion, at least, about the wisdom of a Western movement that was descended from the Enlightenment making common cause with the modernity-loathing jihadists of radical Islam. That discussion is over now. It's impossible, in fact. You can be No Platformed for raising concerns about Islamist extremism.[37] You can be shouted down, heckled, harassed, as ex-Muslim Maryam Namazie was when she criticised Islamic theocracy in a speech at a London university.[38] Even referring to Hamas's attack of 7 October as anti-Semitic, misogynistic and evil might see you accused of that gravest of sins in left circles: Islamophobia.

So the radical feminists at Sisters Uncut say it is 'Islamophobic and racist' to single out Hamas for committing acts of sexual violence on 7 October. That, apparently, is to depict sexual assault 'as an Arab, as opposed to a global, problem'.[39] One left-wing observer describes it as 'triggering' to hear people say that 'Hamas's sole purpose is to kill Jews' – apparently that feeds into the 'Islamophobic tropes' of a 'clash of civilisations' and an 'axis of evil'.[40] Condemning Hamas can even get you blacklisted. Seth Mandel at *Commentary* wrote about 'the insane anti-Jewish literary blacklist', where numerous writers found themselves on a viral left-wing list of moral undesirables simply for objecting to Hamas's pogrom. One writer was included on the list because he had 'lamented the loss of life on 7 October while ignoring the history and reality of Israel's genocidal, apartheid settler state in Palestine'.[41] Lamenting the loss of Jewish life to the knives and guns of anti-Semitic killers – how long before that becomes a fully cancellable offence under the boot of Islamo-leftism?

It was the left's turn against the principles of Enlightenment that made it so lethally susceptible to the 'charms' of radical Islam. Having replaced class politics with identity politics, and its old anti-capitalism with a myopic anti-Westernism, and its one-time commitment to civilisational ideals with a heavy-hearted angst over the 'sins' of our civilisation, the left found itself drawn ever closer to those other haters of everything the West stands for: Islamists.

As Jürgen Habermas has argued, much of what passes for political thought in the modern era is really 'counter-Enlightenment in the garb of post-Enlightenment'.[42] And it was indeed the left's descent into the unlighted caverns of 'counter-Enlightenment', into a new post-class, post-reason politics of identity and division, that led it to the doorstep of radical Islam's radical anti-humanism. As former UK diplomat Sir John Jenkins has put it, 'whatever else may divide them', 'Islamism and the self-styled progressive and postmodern left' share one important thing in common – a burning, sometimes violent urge to 'revolt against modernity'.[43]

The aftershocks of 7 October confirmed how serious the rise of unreason has become. The sight of liberals and leftists marching alongside supporters of Hamas and Islamists who dream of further violence against the Jewish nation will have horrified our Jewish citizens, and it ought to horrify all of us who believe in equality and liberty. A restoration of Enlightenment values is urgently required. Fascism, wherever it comes from, must be forcefully opposed, every time.

ENDNOTES

[1] Labour's Jeremy Corbyn: Why I called Hamas our friends, *Jewish Chronicle*, 14 July 2015

[2] Radical Lives: Mohammed Deif, Novara Media, 27 October 2014

[3] Parting Ways: Jewishness and the Critique of Zionism, *Fathom*, Spring 2013

[4] High on rhetoric, low on solutions, *Weekly Worker*, 19 July 2006

[5] Hamas Covenant, 1988

[6] Does the Tory attack ad take Corbyn's remarks out of context?, *Guardian*, 2 June 2017

[7] Immigration Board of Canada

[8] 'Queers for palestine' must have a death wish, *Telegraph*, 9 November 2023

[9] Don't preach to us, Hamas tells secular West, Reuters, 28 October 2010

[10] The Status of Women in Gaza, IDF, 25 January 2018

[11] Blindness: October 7 and the left, Hadley Freeman, *Jewish Quarterly*, May 2024

[12] Under Cover of War, Human Rights Watch, 20 April 2009

[13] Labour head Corbyn sat on panel alongside Hamas terror leaders in 2012, *Times of Israel*, 20 August 2018

[14] Progressive Anti-Semitism and the Lessons of History, CST, 17 May 2011

[15] Jeremy Corbyn wreath row explained, BBC News, 15 August 2018

[16] Jeremy Corbyn caught on video calling Muslim hate preacher 'honoured citizen' and inviting him to 'tea on the terrace' at the House of Commons, *Daily Mail*, 15 August 2015

[17] Jeremy Corbyn was paid by an Iranian state TV station that was complicit in the forced confession of a tortured journalist, *Business Insider*, 2 July 2016

[18] Briefing on the Muslim Association of Britain, *Workers' Liberty*, 22 August 2006

[19] Former Hamas chief 'behind pro-Palestine Armistice Day protests', *Telegraph*, 6 November 2023

[20] Former Hamas chief 'behind pro-Palestine Armistice Day protests', *Telegraph*, 6 November 2023

[21] In the Party of God, *New Yorker*, 6 October 2002

[22] Professors bullied into silence as students cry transphobia, *The Times*, 17 August 2019

[23] The Postcolonial Left's Blindness to Islamic Homophobia, *Quillette*, 15 November 2023

[24] The Postcolonial Left's Blindness to Islamic Homophobia, *Quillette*, 15 November 2023

[25] The Prophet and the Proletariat, Chris Harman, *International Socialism Journal*, Autumn 1994

[26] The Prophet and the Proletariat, Chris Harman, *International Socialism Journal*, Autumn 1994

[27] *Islamism and the Left*, Policy Exchange, 23 July 2021

[28] An Expedient Alliance? The Muslim Right and the Anglo-American Left, *Dissent*, February 2013

[29] Hammer and Crescent, *New Humanist*, 31 May 2007

[30] Hammer and Crescent, *New Humanist*, 31 May 2007

[31] An Expedient Alliance? The Muslim Right and the Anglo-American Left, *Dissent*, 26 February 2013

[32] Rejoice as Palestinian resistance humiliates racist Israel, *Socialist Worker*, 9 October 2023

[33] Three women convicted of displaying paraglider stickers at London protest, CPS, 13 February 2024

[34] Palestine protesters chant in support of Houthi rebels, *Jewish Chronicle*, 14 January 2024

[35] Pro-terror radical launched 2-hour anti-Israel tirade at Columbia University event weeks before protests exploded: 'Nothing wrong with being a Hamas fighter', *New York Post*, 24 April 2024

[36] In the Party of God, *New Yorker*, 6 October 2002

[37] Anti-racism campaigner 'stopped from speaking at NUS event' over 'Islamophobia' claims, *Guardian*, 18 February 2016

[38] Muslim students try to disrupt ex-Muslim Maryam Namazie's talk on blasphemy at Goldsmiths University, National Secular Society, 3 December 2015

[39] Aren't Palestinians women too?, Sisters Uncut, 2 November 2023

[40] Stop weaponizing the Holocaust, *Hill*, 4 November 2023

[41] The Insane Anti-Jewish Literary Blacklist, *Commentary*, 10 May 2024

[42] *Islamism and the Left*, Policy Exchange, 23 July 2021

[43] *Islamism and the Left*, Policy Exchange, 23 July 2021

SIX

THE CULT OF THE KEFFIYEH

Whatever happened to the sin of cultural appropriation? This ideology of rebuke held sway on university campuses for years. The idea was that no member of the majority group should ever appropriate the cultural habits of a minority group. It's offensive, apparently. It's racial theft. It's parody disguised as authenticity. White men wearing their hair in dreadlocks, white women in kimonos, even gay men twerking or using black slang – all of it was damned as 'stealing', the co-option of the culture of the powerless by the powerful.[1] And yet today, visit any campus in the West and everywhere you look you'll see white youths dressed as Arabs.

Keffiyeh chic is all the rage. You're no one unless you have one of these black-and-white scarves that are widely worn in the Palestinian territories. Student radicals, celebrities, *Guardian*-reading dads on their way for a macchiato – everyone has a keffiyeh draped over their shoulders. It has become the uniform of the politically enlightened, the must-have of the socially aware. They're 'all over Europe', as one writer says; every time there's a 'pro-Palestine' demo you'll be confronted by 'a sea of these garments'.[2] Even the mega-rich are getting in on the act – Balenciaga once made a high-end keffiyeh that will set you back £3,000.[3] But then, you can't put a price on virtue-signalling.

Is this cultural appropriation? If Beyoncé wearing a sari and

Kim Kardashian styling her hair in braids can induce a frenzy of censure among social-justice warriors – as both of those things bizarrely did[4] – then why not bourgeois Westerners pulling on a scarf that has its origins among the nomadic Bedouin tribes of the Arab peninsula?[5] If a student who dons a Mexican sombrero can be branded 'culturally indifferent', then why not a student who wraps himself in Arab cloth?[6] As Julie Burchill has wondered, 'In an age when putting on a sombrero for 60 seconds during a drunken night out at an all-you-can-eat taco bar can be taken as proof of conquistador-level evil… why do these same students swan around wearing the keffiyeh'?[7]

The keffiyeh wearers will say their scarves are about solidarity, not stealing. They're showing their support for a political cause, not purloining Palestinian culture. The reason this scarf is 'worn by non-Palestinians across the world' is 'as a sign of solidarity and allyship', insists *Salon*.[8] But since when did solidarity involve fancy dress? The 1960s students who protested against the Vietnam War did not wear bamboo conical hats in mimicry of the Vietnamese peasants who so often felt the heat of America's bombs and napalm. Western supporters of the Quit India movement were not known for wearing white dhotis in the style of Mahatma Gandhi. Solidarity was expressed with words and actions, not imitation of style.

No, there is something else going on with the cult of the keffiyeh, something that falls outside of the traditional realm of solidarity and even awareness-raising. That an item of clothing has become so omnipresent among the virtuous set, that the activist class covets this scarf with such relish that there has been an 'influx of mass-produced keffiyehs' into our societies,[9] points to a performative streak in pro-Palestine activism. That it has become *de rigueur* in certain circles to flout all the laws of 'cultural appropriation' and pull on this 'hot accessory [of] the West' – as the *Guardian* calls it – suggests the activist set is as keen to say something about itself and its own rectitude as it is about the predicament of the Palestinian people. That so many progressives rarely leave the house without first wrapping themselves in a keffiyeh confirms the extent to which the Palestine question itself has come to be wrapped up in the personalities of these influencers, in their sense of self, in their very social status.

The cult of the keffiyeh is proof that Palestine has become, in the words of Jake Wallis Simons, the great 'social signifier' of the radically chic of the Western world. Pitying Palestine, and by extension hating Israel, has become a 'core part of a suite of views held by the progressives who set the tenor of much of our culture', he says.[10] It has become the 'luxury belief' *du jour*, the means by which one's social worth is measured. This goes way beyond 'cultural appropriation' – it is the wholesale moral appropriation of an entire people and their plight by the political intimates of high society with virtue to advertise.

Keffiyeh chic has been bubbling and brewing for some time. For Palestinians the scarf has been a symbol of resistance since the 1930s, when Palestinian *fedayeen* (guerillas) started launching attacks on the British rulers of what was then known as Mandatory Palestine. The fighters donned the keffiyeh in order to erase any 'markers of identity' between them, says cultural historian Jane Tynan: whether you were a bourgeois or a peasant who had opted to take up arms against the British, you wore the keffiyeh, making you equals.[11] The keffiyeh exploded into global view in the 1960s with the founding of the Palestine Liberation Organisation by Yasser Arafat and others. Arafat was rarely seen without a keffiyeh draping from his head down his back.

The 1969 photo of Palestinian terrorist Leila Khaled wearing a keffiyeh and holding an AK47 was the thing that really ensured the fame – or infamy – of this item of desert headgear. Khaled was the first woman ever to hijack an airplane, TWA Flight 840 from Rome to Tel Aviv, which she did with her fellow militants in the Popular Front for the Liberation of Palestine. Visions of this 25-year-old wearing a keffiyeh over her hair were beamed around the world, 'catapult[ing] the keffiyeh into Western consciousness', says Niloufar Haidari.[12] The first keffiyeh craze started in earnest. Western radicals wore it as evidence of their edginess. There were handwringing debates about 'terrorist chic' and the troubling possibility that some youths think 'terrorism is cool'.[13]

In later decades the keffiyeh became a fashion statement of general angst, of a moderate anarchic sentiment, rarely having anything much to do with Palestine. The media's description of a squatter who was evicted from a pub owned by Gordon Ramsay summed up the sort of people who wore it – he was 'dressed in a bucket hat, keffiyeh face covering and carrying a skateboard'.[14] Virtually every stall in Camden Market sold them. It had well and truly become a 'commodity of resistance aesthetics', in the words of media professor Robert G White.[15] Soon it was on the catwalks. We've had 'peasant glamour' and 'hobo style' – now behold 'urban combat with a Middle Eastern twist', wrote fashion critic Charlie

Porter in 2001, when the keffiyeh became a must-have again. Belgian fashion designer Raf Simons sent male models down the runway in keffiyehs and 'skinny black drainpipes and bulky army surplus coats' – a 'fiery symbol', the fashion press gushed.[16]

It featured in the fashion shows of Galliano, Balenciaga and Louis Vuitton. David Beckham, Colin Farrell and Mary-Kate Olsen took to wearing it. Urban Outfitters stocked them (but later withdrew them following complaints).[17] Even Carrie Bradshaw on *Sex and the City* wore a 'keffiyeh boob tube' at one point.[18] From being the headwear of female hijackers to the statement top of Western culture's best-known single girl – such was the curious journey of this old sartorial staple of the Bedouin.

And now the keffiyeh is back. Since Hamas's pogrom of 7 October, 'urban combat with a twist of Middle Eastern' has become the look once more in socially aware circles. You declare your pronouns, you take the knee and you wear a keffiyeh. And this time, apparently, it's not fashion, it's politics. It's not style, it's solidarity. It's no mere 'fiery symbol' – it's a fiery statement of one's deep convictions about Israel / Palestine. And it certainly isn't cultural appropriation. As CNN somewhat defensively explained, 'non-Palestinians should be careful when wearing the keffiyeh in the traditional style worn by Bedouins', and should always do their 'research about the garment before wearing it', but, generally speaking, putting on a keffiyeh can be a 'great show of solidarity'.[19]

The hypocrisy is something else. This is the same CNN that threw its corporate weight behind the cultural-appropriation panic. Which published pieces with headlines like 'Dear white people with dreadlocks: some things to consider' and 'Dear white gay men: stop stealing black female culture'.[20] It's the same CNN whose writers raged against 'blackfishing', which apparently is when 'white entertainers' appear to be 'imitating the appearance of black people'.[21] It's the same CNN which sternly reminded the good people of the United States that cultural appropriation is 'when people with power and privilege take customs and traditions that oppressed people have long been marginalised for and repurpose them as a hot new thing'.[22]

That might just be the best description of the fad for keffiyeh-wearing: people with privilege (Ivy League radicals, the laptop elites, latte socialists) taking a custom of a foreign people (the Bedouin and the Palestinians) and turning it into the 'hot new thing' – as the *Guardian* says, the keffiyeh truly has been 'cemented... as a hot item'.[23]

To many of us, 'cultural appropriation' was always a cranky, illiberal idea. It was the elite policing of people's cultural and clothing choices. At its worst, it was dangerously racially divisive, with its hectoring instruction that we all 'stay in our racial lane' and never dabble in the fashions and ideas of ethnic groups supposedly less privileged than our own. And yet it is striking that the liberal establishment's patrician 'Dear White People' missives dried up completely in the face of the latest keffiyeh craze. As Michael Deacon of the *Telegraph* has said, it might be nice if the overlords of correct cultural behaviour would let us know when they 'decide to make abrupt changes to the rules they've sought to impose upon society'. In this case, he says, they might have said: 'ATTENTION ALL CITIZENS: Cultural appropriation is no longer considered a heinous offence against marginalised and oppressed minorities. Instead, it is now considered a noble expression of solidarity with them. Please update your records accordingly.'[24]

Clearly, a calculation has been made by the cultural establishment. It has decided that in the case of the keffiyeh, more status points can be accrued through the wearing of it than through the policing of its wearing. One's moral position is fortified and even improved more by the donning of this customary garb of an 'oppressed people' than by the reproaching of its cultural appropriation. That those who wear the keffiyeh have entirely escaped the charge of cultural appropriation confirms how useful this garment is to the activist class, how central it has become to their daily displays of righteousness. That we live in an era of such madness that white women can be rebuked for wearing hoop earrings, and gay men can be reprimanded for saying 'Yass', and universities will issue guidelines on what it is 'appropriate' to wear on Halloween, and yet the armies of bourgeois youths in Bedouin headgear get a free pass, is a testament to the sainted nature of the keffiyeh in virtuous circles.[25]

And what is its usefulness? What holy service does this garment play in the lives of the elites? Its prime role is as a signifier of virtue. It is sartorial shorthand for ethical correctness. It communicates to your fellow travellers in the universe of luxury beliefs that you, too, have contempt for Israel and compassion for Palestine – an entirely requisite credo for access to the cultural establishment in the 21st century. Wearing the keffiyeh in public, or posting photos online of yourself wrapped up in one, is fundamentally a statement of your moral fitness for political high society. Far from being an act of solidarity, keffiyeh-wearing is more about raising awareness of yourself, and your goodness, than it is about raising awareness of the Palestinians and their challenges.

Indeed, you can wear the keffiyeh while knowing next to nothing about the part of the world it comes from. Potkin Azarmehr, the Iranian writer who fled Iran for the UK following the Islamic Revolution of 1979, has noted the 'ignorance' of many of the keffiyeh-wearing agitators against Israel on the streets of our cities. There is a 'startling disconnect', he says, 'between their strong opinions on the Gaza conflict and their shaky grasp of basic facts about it'. The keffiyeh classes 'seem eager to make excuses for Hamas', but they are 'conspicuously uninformed about exactly what or who this terrorist group represents'. He gives the example of Queers for Palestine, who 'flirt with justifying Hamas's atrocities', which is 'bewildering' given that Hamas's Islamist ideology is 'clearly antithetical to the rights and values these groups claim to champion'. Hamas's 'reactionary agenda', says Azarmehr, is 'profoundly hostile to women's rights and LGBT individuals'.[26]

That the keffiyeh set can be staggeringly ignorant of the backwardness and barbarism of Hamas, that they can wear a Palestinian symbol while being utterly unlettered on the present realities of life in Palestine, confirms that this garment is a signifier of feeling more than knowledge. Indeed, a post-pogrom survey of US students, those most likely to be adorned in the keffiyeh, uncovered an alarmingly frail grasp on the fundamental facts of the Middle East. For instance, only 47 per cent of the students who regularly chant the infamous slogan, 'From the river to the sea, Palestine will be free', were able to name the river and the sea it references. Some thought it referred to the Nile and the Euphrates. Others to the Caribbean. Some thought 'the sea' was a reference to the Dead Sea, which is a lake. Less than a quarter of the students knew who Yasser Arafat was. More than 10 per cent thought he was the first prime minister of Israel. Mercifully, when shown a map of the Middle East, and informed that having a Palestinian state stretching from the Jordan River to the Mediterranean Sea would leave 'no room for Israel', many of the students downgraded their support for the 'river to the sea' slogan from 'would chant' to 'probably not'.[27]

Think about this: radical youths wear the keffiyeh without knowing *where it comes from*. Without knowing that it was between the Jordan and the Mediterranean, not in the Caribbean, that the *fedayeen* first wore the keffiyeh as a symbol of resistance, and where Yasser Arafat, who was never the prime minister of Israel, made it a core part of his wardrobe. Again, the cultural-appropriation panic comes to mind. *GQ* once ridiculed the white appropriators of Native American garb and white men with dreadlocks as 'utterly ignorant' – 'ignorant of a minority culture's journey and historical suffering'.[28] It slammed the 'pale, sickly millennials' who know nothing of the cultures they steal. And yet not a word of such salty criticism has been raised against the TikTok revolutionaries of the Ivy League who wear the keffiyeh without knowing where Palestine is or what Hamas does. The definition of 'ignorance', surely, is Queers for Palestine wearing keffiyehs while being blissfully unaware that if they ever set foot in Gaza their pronouns would be was / were quicker than they could say 'Free Palestine'.[29]

The keffiyeh classes don't only have a 'startling disconnect' from the realities of the Middle East, but also from the true global injustices of the 21st century. Consider where their keffiyehs are likely to come from – China. The great paradox of the cult of the keffiyeh is that, as Niloufar Haidari reports, 'the more popular the keffiyeh has become in the West, the less this has translated into a boon for the Palestinian economy'. There is only *one* Palestinian weavery left that makes keffiyehs. The keffiyehs we see in the coffee shops, campuses and art galleries of the West are 'mass-produced' items 'from China'. The last remaining keffiyeh-maker in the Palestinian territories says it has become 'increasingly difficult to compete with the low prices of the imported counterfeits'.[30] That the keffiyeh craze of the Western bourgeoisie has hurt keffiyeh-makers in Palestine is a dark irony that will not be lost on those of us who know that the virtue-signalling of the powerful often has unintended consequences.

The 'Made in China' radicalism of the keffiyeh classes is commodified resistance summed up. Nothing better captures the moral unworldliness of the pro-Palestine set than the fact that their sartorial signifiers of status were likely made by hyper-exploited workers in the world's largest unfree state. That the scarves they put on to show how much they care for Palestine were likely weaved by people who lack the fundamental rights of freedom of speech and democratic enfranchisement. That their noisy displays of moral concern for Palestine are being facilitated by poorly paid weavers in an authoritarian state for whom their moral concern is thin indeed, if not non-existent. It is even possible that Uyghurs made their keffiyehs, given that tens of thousands from this repressed people have been compelled by the Chinese regime to work in factories, including textile factories.[31] Western youths signifying their pain for the oppressed state of Palestine with garments made by genuinely oppressed Uyghurs is surely the most late-stage capitalism thing that has ever happened.

The commodified concern for Palestine over and above every other wrong in the world – including the wrongs visited on the serfs who make the keffiyehs the wealthy wear – speaks to how important luxury beliefs, a term coined by author Rob Henderson, have become to the new elites. As Matthew Goodwin explains, where the 'old elite' derived its sense of social status from 'physical manifestations of wealth, such as fine clothes, jewellery, foreign travel, servants, private carriages and large properties', the new elite tends to distinguish itself from the 'low-status' masses by 'focus[ing] far more on projecting their "cultural capital" rather than their "economic capital"'. With prosperity 'spread far more widely across society' than was the case in the past, 'ostentatious displays of riches have much less significance'. Instead, says Goodwin, 'for the sophisticated, financially secure, urban-dwelling, university-educated new elite', a certain set of 'fashionable beliefs has become the new signifier of social status'.[32] And chief among them, even more so post-pogrom, is pity for Palestine, combined with dread of Israel. The keffiyeh has become the material expression of this luxury belief. Thus did the headgear of desert-dwelling peasants become the main means through which the rich of the West demonstrate their moral capital and social status. Is *that* 'cultural appropriation'?

That the keffiyeh has become a means of moral distinction, a part of the cultural armoury that allows the luxury moralists to 'distinguish themselves from the "low status" masses', represents a total negation of what this garment once meant to Palestinians.[33] Where, in Jane Tynan's words, the keffiyeh was first adopted by the *fedayeen* to erase any 'markers of identity' between them, now it *is* a marker of identity. Now it is a tool not for burying class differences, but for accentuating them, for saying: 'I care for Palestine and thus my status is higher than yours.'

In this way, the cult of the keffiyeh is yet another form of 'radical chic', to use the term created by Tom Wolfe in his still blistering 1970 essay, 'Radical Chic: That Party at Lenny's'. Taking as his starting point a fundraising party for the Black Panthers that composer Leonard Bernstein held in his opulent apartment in Manhattan, Wolfe mused on how, at certain points in history, the self-styled enlightened elite develops an intense resentment for the 'striving' working class and instead finds itself drawn towards a 'romanticised identification with the seemingly primitive lower classes'.[34] That is, they distinguish themselves from the working masses through adopting a refined concern for the hyper-oppressed. And since radical chic 'is only radical in style', wrote Wolfe, 'in its heart it is part of Society and its traditions' of social climbing.[35] It is an alignment with oppression that in reality advances privilege.

As British art writer Michael Bracewell put it in his 2004 essay, 'Molotov Cocktails', Wolfe had diagnosed a trend whereby the 'patrician classes' seek to 'luxuriate in both a vicarious glamour and a monopoly on virtue through their public espousal of street politics: a politics, moreover, of minorities so removed from their sphere of experience and so absurdly, diametrically opposed to the islands of privilege on which the cultural aristocracy maintain their isolation, that the whole basis of their relationship is wildly out of kilter from the start'.[36] This is the keffiyeh classes, too: ostentatiously identifying with an 'oppressed people', not to better understand that people's pain, or to fashion solutions for its easing, but to fortify their own cultural aristocracy at home.

In other ways, though, keffiyeh chic is worse than radical chic. The Lenny Bernsteins of the world might be forgiven for feeling drawn to the drive and passion of 'street' movements like the Black Panthers. They must have seemed exciting to an ageing composer in his lonely, cavernous Manhattan flat. The keffiyeh classes, in contrast, are attracted to the Palestinian people not for their dynamism, but for their wretchedness. Not for their vim but for their victimisation. Where the elite posturing that Wolfe so mercilessly ribbed was 'vicarious radicalism', the cult of the keffiyeh is something far more unpleasant: vicarious victimhood.

The keffiyeh classes seem keen to 'appropriate' not only the clothing of the Palestinians, but their suffering, too. Witness the organisers of the Gaza encampment at Columbia University in New York City mimicking both Palestinian style and Palestinian privation. One student leader said she and her comrades were going hungry and required 'humanitarian aid'. Do you want us to die of dehydration and starvation?, she asked university bosses.[37] In a viral clip, a group of keffiyeh-wearing students was seen receiving 'humanitarian aid' through the college gates.[38] I say humanitarian aid – it was probably a Starbucks order and blueberry muffins from a nearby bodega. Here we had privileged youths on an Ivy League campus cosplaying as victims of a humanitarian crisis; comfortably off Ivy Leaguers masquerading as the wretched of the Earth.

It provided a grim insight into the true nature of 'Palestine solidarity'. It shone a light on why so many of our young chant, 'In our thousands, in our millions, we are all Palestinians'. This is a new and unsettling form of activism. It is not 1960s-style solidarity with foreign struggles or even radical chic, that old politics as fashion. No, it is a coveting of suffering. The keffiyeh classes, it seems to me, crave the moral rush of oppression, the thrill of persecution. They pull on the garb of a beleaguered people in order to escape, however fleetingly, the pampered reality of their own lives. In order to taste that most prized of social assets in the woke era: victimhood. In draping the keffiyeh around their shoulders, they get to be someone else for a while. Someone less bourgeois, less white. Someone a little more exotic, a little more interesting. It's less politics than therapy. They seek to wash away the 'sin' of their privilege through mimicking what they consider to be the least privileged people on Earth. That's what the keffiyeh has become: the cloth with which the rich seek to scrub away their white guilt.

If the keffiyeh is the uniform of this Palestine politics of victimhood, then its currency is images of Palestinian suffering. Where yesteryear's purveyors of radical chic revelled in images of revolting minorities, today's followers of the cult of the keffiyeh savour images of Palestinian destitution. They trade in photos of Palestinian pain, meaning that social media has become 'oversaturated with traumatic imagery', as one writer describes it.

Log on and you'll be instantly exposed to a 'kaleidoscopic view of human suffering without respite'.[39] Not content with commodifying Palestinian attire, they commodify Palestinian trauma, too. They make a spectacle of Palestinian agony. Not to assist Palestinains in any meaningful way – how could it? – but rather to inflame their own satisfying feelings of collective moral revulsion.

Even requests from Palestinians to stop sharing horrific images from their wars have not been enough to slow this grim trade. A few years ago, Palestinian psychiatrist Samah Jabr counselled Westerners against sharing 'shocking content' showing 'shattered people' in the Palestinian territories, on the basis that such 'pictures of pain' violate 'the privacy and dignity of the subjects' and can 'create terror' among Palestinians who might fear suffering the same fate. These images might 'provide thrills' to outside observers, and nurture 'more "likes" and "shares"' online, but they can be devastating to 'public morale' in the Palestinian territories, Jabr wrote.[40] It was a fruitless plea. Imagery of Palestinian suffering is too valuable to the keffiyeh classes to be sacrificed to trifling concerns about Palestinian dignity. Your pain is ours now, just like your headwear.

The elites' vicarious victimhood through the Palestine drama is a dangerous game. It seems undeniable now that the more the cultural powers of the West crave and collect depictions of Palestinian distress, the more the ideologues of Hamas will be willing to supply such depictions. Witness Yahya Sinwar's insistence, in the summarising words of CNN, that the 'spiralling civilian death toll in Gaza' will likely 'work in [Hamas's] favour'. Sinwar, the military leader of Hamas in Gaza, callously describes the deaths of Palestinians as 'necessary sacrifices' to get the Israelis 'right where we want them.'[41]

Hamas clearly recognises that when the cultural establishments of global capitalism treat every image of Palestinian death as an indictment of Israeli evil, when the West's activist class, media elites and online influencers hold up every picture of a broken Palestinian as proof of the Jewish State's 'uniquely murderous' nature,[42] then it is in Hamas's interests to prolong the war and allow more such suffering to occur. Having made Palestinian agony the currency of their activism, the activist class cannot now feign surprise at Hamas's willingness to let this disastrous war continue. Hamas's intransigence in the face of its far more powerful foe is a direct consequence of the keffiyeh classes' commodification of Palestinian pain as a testament to both Israeli malfeasance and Western indifference.

The cult of victimhood's greatest offence is to reduce everything to a simplistic clash between the oppressed and the oppressor, good and evil, light and dark. This movement requires not only victims it might ostentatiously empathise with, but also the opposite: *victimisers,* the monsters of persecution, who must be noisily raged at. As Professor Joshua Berman writes, the 'Palestinian ideology of victimhood… constructs a struggle between a victim-hero in opposition to a scapegoat'. And this can lead to a 'revelling in caricatured depictions of the oppressor', he says. So where Palestinian radicals 'traffic in classic hook-nose anti-Semitic tropes', their Western supporters traffic in the insistence that the Jewish State is uniquely murderous, given to bloodletting, obsessed with murdering children, and so on.[43] This is the thin line between pity and hate. Pity for Palestinians morphs with frightening ease into hatred for the world's only Jewish nation, courtesy of the morally infantile narrative the cultural establishment has weaved around this most fraught of conflicts.

The end result? Protesters in keffiyehs telling Jews in New York City to 'go back to Poland'.[44] Activists in keffiyehs shouting on the NY subway: 'Raise your hand if you're a Zionist'.[45] Britons in keffiyehs marching alongside radical Islamists who long for further pogroms against the Jewish State.[46] The aftermath of 7 October is a painful reminder that the facile moral binaries of identity politics are far more likely to resuscitate racism than tackle it.

ENDNOTES

[1] Let's Talk About White Gays 'Stealing Black Female Culture', *Cut*, 15 July 2014

[2] Your £800 Palestinian keffiyeh does not say what you think it says, *Standard*, 25 April 2024

[3] Your £800 Palestinian keffiyeh does not say what you think it says, *Standard*, 25 April 2024

[4] Why Beyoncé and Coldplay's Latest Music Video Is an Example of Cultural Appropriation, *Teen Vogue*, 31 January 2016; Kim Kardashian West is Being Called Out for Wearing Braids (Again), *Teen Vogue*, 3 March 2020

[5] What is a keffiyeh, who wears it, and how did it become a symbol for Palestinians?, NPR, 6 December 2023

[6] Student union bans 'racist' sombreros, *Guardian*, 29 September 2015

[7] The cultural appropriation of the keffiyeh, *Spectator*, 4 November 2023

[8] How the keffiyeh became a Palestinian symbol of resistance, *Salon*, 1 May 2024

[9] From Yasser Arafat to Madonna: how the Palestinian keffiyeh became a global symbol, *Guardian*, 11 December 2023

[10] *Israelophobia: The Newest Version of the Oldest Hatred and What To Do About It*, Jake Wallis Simons, Constable, 2023

[11] From Yasser Arafat to Madonna: how the Palestinian keffiyeh became a global symbol, *Guardian*, 11 December 2023

[12] From Yasser Arafat to Madonna: how the Palestinian keffiyeh became a global symbol, *Guardian*, 11 December 2023

[13] *Symbolism in Terrorism: Motivation, Communication, and Behavior*, Jonathan Matusitz, Rowan and Littlefield, 2014

[14] Squatters slowly filter out of Gordon Ramsay's pub, *Peterborough Matters*, 19 April 2024

[15] *An Atonal Cinema: Resistance, Counterpoint and Dialogue in Transnational Palestine*, Robert G White, Bloomsbury Academic, 2023

[16] What a riot, *Guardian*, 6 July 2001

[17] Is the war over for terrorist chic?, *Irish Independent*, 8 November 2008

[18] Identity, Tradition, Resistance: The Keffiyeh Explained, *Vogue*, 2 May 2024

[19] The keffiyeh explained: How this scarf became a Palestinian national symbol, CNN, 28 November 2023

[20] Black writer's plea to white gay men, CNN, 4 November 2014

[21] What 'Blackfishing' means and why people do it, CNN, 8 July 2021

[22] What 'Blackfishing' means and why people do it, CNN, 8 July 2021

[23] From Yasser Arafat to Madonna: how the Palestinian keffiyeh became a global symbol, *Guardian*, 11 December 2023

[24] These anti-Israel student protests lay bare the brazen hypocrisy of the woke Left, *Telegraph*, 7 May 2024

[25] University memo addresses appropriateness of Halloween costumes, *Daily Princetonian*, 31 October 2023

[26] The staggering ignorance of the 'pro-Palestine' protesters, *spiked*, 2 June 2024

[27] From Which River to Which Sea?, *Wall Street Journal*, 5 December 2023

[28] Cultural appropriation is about being utterly ignorant, *GQ*, 13 October 2018

[29] 'Queers for Palestine' must have a death wish, *Telegraph*, 9 November 2023

[30] From Yasser Arafat to Madonna: how the Palestinian keffiyeh became a global symbol, *Guardian*, 11 December 2023

[31] China: 83 major brands implicated in report on forced labour of ethnic minorities from Xinjiang assigned to factories across provinces; Includes company responses, Business & Human Rights Resource Centre, 1 March 2020

[32] Rise of the Luxury Belief Class, Matt Goodwin Substack, 9 October 2023

[33] Rise of the Luxury Belief Class, Matt Goodwin Substack, 9 October 2023

[34] See *Postwar American Fiction and the Rise of Modern Conservatism*, Bryan M Santin, Cambridge University Press, 2021

[35] *Radical Chic and Mau-Mauing the Flak Catchers*, Tom Wolfe, Farrar, Straus and Giroux, 1970

[36] Molotov Cocktails, *Frieze*, 11 November 2004

[37] Columbia University's protesters' most moronic moments: From demanding 'humanitarian aid' to complaining about their privacy and whining when the cops finally cracked down, *Daily Mail*, 1 May 2024

[38] Columbia University student crumbles under questioning after claiming school was 'blocking their access to food and water' and demanding 'humanitarian aid', *Daily Mail*, 1 May 2024

[39] Is the Flood of Graphic Imagery From Gaza Warping Our Perception of War?, *New Republic*, 5 December 2023

[40] Permissible pain: How to deal with traumatic images coming from Palestine, *Middle East Monitor*, 24 May 2021

[41] Hamas leader said civilian death toll could benefit militant group in Gaza war, WSJ reports, CNN, 11 June 2024

[42] Who will shine a light on the atrocities in Gaza if all the journalists are wiped out?, *Guardian*, 29 November 2023

[43] Blacks, Palestinians and the Disastrous Politics of Rage, *Aish*

[44] Have we learned nothing? The protester's taunt, 'Go back to Poland,' is grotesque, *LA Times*, 6 May 2024

[45] Protesters Chant 'Raise Your Hand If You're a Zionist' on Manhattan Subway, Yahoo! News, 12 June 2024

[46] Racism in the mask of anti-imperialism, *spiked*, 29 October 2023

SEVEN

AGAINST SAFETY

So, we live in an era when you can be banished from a university for saying women don't have penises, but you'll be fine if you say 'kill all Jews'. We live in a time when asking someone where they're from is considered a 'racial microaggression', but hollering 'Globalise the intifada' in the aftermath of an 'intifada' in which a thousand Jews were slaughtered is apparently okay. We live in a culture in which students will demand access to 'safe spaces', complete with colouring books and bean bags, if a speaker they hate turns up on campus. And yet these same students who fear words like the rest of us fear death will happily cheer the invasion of Israel and the murder of hundreds of its citizens. No safe space for Jews, it seems.

This was one of the most unsettling revelations in the aftermath of the 7 October pogrom: that snowflakes have a secret genocidal streak. That student activists who wail about being 'erased' if you fail to use their preferred pronouns don't seem to have much of a problem with the literal erasure of the citizens of the Jewish State.

Overnight, students who had bristled at such 'microaggressions' as 'Don't you want a family?' – it's an act of unforgivable 'heteronormativity', apparently, to assume everyone wants a family[1] – were gloating over the massacre of entire families in southern Israel. It was just two weeks after the pogrom that some students at George Washington University in Washington, DC projected that slogan, 'Glory to our martyrs', on to the exterior of a campus building.[2] That is, glory to the mobs that had lately invaded the Jewish nation to rape and massacre innocents.

This is a university whose list of microaggressions includes asking an Asian person to help you with a maths problem (that's an act of 'implicit bias', apparently) and using the phrase, 'When I look at you, I don't see colour' (this mini-outrage 'denies a person of colour's racial / ethnic experiences', it seems).[3] Students who had expected protection from normal, everyday conversation were suddenly glorying in one of the worst acts of violence of modern times. A campus on which asking an Asian student to assist you with an equation is considered a sly act of racial judgement found itself coated in a slogan that celebrated the visceral racism of the pogromists of Hamas.

In the aftermath of the pogrom, George Washington was rocked by protests that were outright pro-Hamas. At one, the student mob chanted 'We will honour all our martyrs!'.[4] This is a university where the nickname of the sports teams had to be changed because the student body found it so existentially offensive. What was it? 'Colonials.' Earlier in 2023, pre-7 October, the 'campus community' at George Washington demanded a 'reckoning' with the 'fraught history' of this hurtful nickname. It is 'entangled', they said, with 'violence towards Native Americans and other colonised people.'[5] And yet just months later, they were saying, essentially, 'We will honour Hamas'. Students who had felt so wounded by a word were taking pleasure in the literal wounding of Jews.

George Washington is a campus that has a 'rape-culture awareness committee'. It's a campus where students write pained articles about the 'unwanted sexual advances' they experience.[6] And yet now some in that same student community were openly 'honouring' an army of anti-Semites that had visited apocalyptic violence on the women of southern Israel. Being badly flirted with by a drunken jock in the student bar is an intolerable instance of 'rape culture',[7] apparently, but the collective brutalisation of Jewish women by the misogynists of Hamas is something to be 'honoured'.

Campuses across the US were shaken by a 'rape panic' in recent years, as some critical feminists referred to it.[8] There was a culture of 'sexual paranoia', said Laura Kipnis in her explosive book, *Unwanted Advances: Sexual Paranoia Comes to Campus*.[9] All sorts of male behaviour, from the genuinely bad to the clumsy and even the innocent, were reimagined as 'rape culture' in action. The definition of 'sexual assault' was expanded to include not only actual assault, but also 'the male gaze' – or 'an accidental bump, a touch on a shoulder, an unwanted invitation, an attempted kiss, hugging...'[10] The truth behind all this sexual paranoia was that the incidence of rape and actual sexual assault on campuses in the US was lower than in the general population. As one writer summed it up: 'The rate of rape and sexual assault was 1.2 times higher for non-students (7.6 per 1,000) than for students (6.1 per 1,000).'[11]

And yet these sexual paranoiacs of the 21st-century campus who once saw rape everywhere refused to see it where it really existed: in the burnt-out, body-strewn hellscape of southern Israel following Hamas's invasion. These campus radicals have given a 'free pass to Hamas's shameful [violence]', wrote Thomas L Friedman. They seem positively blasé, he said, about the fact that Hamas 'raped Israeli women'.[12] Students at the University of Pennsylvania invited to their campus a 'solidarity activist' who had tweeted 'Glad Hamas killed that bitch' in response to a photo of a 22-year-old woman who was murdered at the Nova music festival during the pogrom.[13] The kind of activists who'd once taken such fright at a man's hand on their shoulder were now rubbing shoulders with a man who had saluted the murder of a Jewish woman.

Some student activists even descended on the offices of the *New York Times* to decry its 'reporting [of] Hamas rapes'.[14] The students of the Palestinian Youth Movement[15] took over the lobby of the *New York Times* and even blocked its printing facilities in Queens. They damned the paper as 'The New York War Crimes'. Its offence? Covering Hamas's acts of sexual violence on 7 October. These rape stories are 'lies', said the leaflet the protesters handed out.[16] The kind of activists who just a few years ago might have encouraged young women to 'tell their truth' about the awfulness of life under 'the male gaze' were now trying to physically prevent a newspaper from telling the truth about Hamas's crimes against womankind.[17]

As we've already seen, at Harvard University on 7 October, even before the pogrom had ended, 31 student societies published a letter saying Israel was 'entirely responsible' for all the 'unfolding violence'.[18] Even as women and children were being murdered, these privileged Ivy Leaguers some 5,000 miles from the slaughter zone were absolving the murderers of responsibility. The victim of the pogrom – Israel – is 'the only one to blame', they said. This is a university that has 'safe spaces' in which students can seek refuge from the supposed hardships of everyday conversation. Spaces in which there are 'massage circles' and special time for the 'processing and journaling' of difficult feelings.[19] And yet upon hearing of one of the worst hardships of our time – the pogrom – some Harvard students essentially said: 'You had it coming.'

At British universities, too, anti-Israel rage was widespread. At some of the protests, students chanted 'Globalise the intifada!' and scoffed at concerns that 'some Jews see [this as] a genocidal call'.[20] It is a scoffing that might have carried more weight if it hadn't come from the kind of officious campus leftists who spent the past 20 years banning everything they dislike on the basis that it might incite violence. One UK students' union banned Eminem's music on the grounds that it is anti-gay and misogynistic.[21] Numerous universities banned the Robin Thicke song, 'Blurred Lines', because its lyrics 'undermine and degrade women'.[22] Students' unions routinely 'No Platform' certain speakers, silencing not only genuine extremists, but also gender-critical feminists, due to their scandalous belief that men are not women.

That Britain's snowflake student activists who dread white rap and live in fear of 'TERFs' were happy to chant for further 'intifadas' in the weeks following an intifada in which a thousand Jews were murdered was yet more proof of the tidal wave of cant that swept Anglo-American campuses after 7 October. Students who scurry to their 'safe space' upon hearing 'My Name Is' or Helen Joyce saying people with penises are men were suddenly comfortable with chanting for the globalisation of violence. For that's what an intifada is – a violent uprising against the Jewish State, or, let's be frank, against Jews.

The student world's overnight shift from craving safety to praising pogroms was extraordinary. For years, student activists were known, and often pilloried, for their hyper-fragility. For seeking sanctuary in safe spaces when such 'dangerous' speakers as Christina Hoff Sommers or Ben Shapiro showed up.[23] For hiding in specially designated safety zones, complete with Play-Doh, colouring books and calming music, upon discovering that a critical feminist was coming to campus to criticise the idea of 'rape culture'.[24] For requiring 'de-stressing' animals that they might hold and pet whenever they felt full of angst. At Cambridge University in the UK, 'guinea pigs, a three-legged cat and several dogs' were made available to the student body.[25] A Jack Russell terrier called Twiglet had to be retired from de-stressing duties after so many angst-ridden students insisted on petting him that 'the pooch was left exhausted'.[26]

Students demanded constant psychic safety. Safety from difficult ideas, controversial texts, unsettling images. At Cambridge, 'trigger warnings' were added to Shakespeare's plays, informing students that they might feel distressed by the material within. Students were forewarned that seminars on *Titus Andronicus* would include 'discussion of sexual violence [and] sexual assault'.[27] From fearing scenes of sexual assault in Shakespeare to ignoring acts of sexual assault in Israel – it's been a journey.

'Safetyism', writes psychologist Pamela B Paresky, had become the dominant 'moral culture' on campus. 'Perceived safety' had become a 'sacred value'. And yet, in the aftermath of 7 October, she says, the supposed protections of 'safetyism' were flagrantly denied to Jewish students. They, and they alone, were 'expected to face the discomfort of hateful speech'.[28] Student activists who for years had demanded emotional protection from biological truth, rude rap and even the Bard now expected Jewish students to hear chants about 'intifada' and Hamas's 'glorious martyrs' day in, day out.

In fact, they expected Jews to hear even worse. Soon came the 'Gaza encampments'. At Columbia, George Washington, Harvard, Pennsylvania, University College London, Warwick and other universities in the US and the UK, students set up 'tent communities' to register their fury with Israel's war in Gaza. The thinness of the line between so-called anti-Zionism and anti-Semitism had never been more apparent. At the Columbia camp, a placard denounced the Jewish nation as the 'pigs of the Earth'.[29] 'We don't want no two states / We want '48', students chanted, clearly dreaming of that era when the modern state of Israel did not yet exist.[30] Jewish students were harassed. Some were told to 'Go back to Poland'. A protester in a keffiyeh held up a sign with an arrow pointing at a group of Jews and describing them as Hamas's 'next targets'.[31] Campus activists who wrung their hands over the microaggression of asking someone 'Where are you from?' were now wishing death on Jews.[32]

Jewish students at Pennsylvania were told to go back to 'fucking Berlin where you came from'.[33] Penn acknowledged a rise in outright anti-Semitism on campus, including the daubing of 'swastikas and hateful graffiti' on university property, as well as 'chants at rallies… that glorify the terrorist atrocities of Hamas, that celebrate and praise the slaughter and kidnapping of innocent people, and that question Israel's very right to exist'.[34] A protester at George Washington held a placard showing the Palestinian flag and that most chilling slogan of the 20th century: 'Final Solution'.[35] At Exeter University in the UK, Jewish students fled campus after being surrounded by a mob of a hundred angry Israelophobes.[36] It feels, wrote Noah Rubin at the *New York Post*, that our 'elite schools' are turning into 'Hamas University'.[37]

The dark irony of 'Hamas University' is that it was the handiwork of an activist class that has spent recent years fretting over the 'alt-right'. Every time a Proud Boy or a Milo Yiannopoulos arrived on a campus, student radicals would say: 'There is no room for fascism.'[38] Yet just years later this same station of self-styled 'anti-fascists' had nurtured a truly fascistic climate. One in which Jews were told to go back to Europe, swastikas were painted on walls, and there was dreaming everywhere one looked of the coming destruction of the Jewish nation.

The thing that truly exposed the hollow piousness, the shameless double standards, of the modern-day academic elite was the infamous Congressional hearing where the presidents of three of America's top universities were grilled on anti-Semitism. It was December 2023, two months after the pogrom. Liz Magill, president of Penn, Claudine Gay, then president of Harvard, and Sally Kornbluth, president of the Massachusetts Institute of Technology (MIT), were questioned by Elise Stefanik, a Republican representative for New York. Someone calling for a 'genocide of Jews' – would that 'violate [your] rules on bullying and harassment?', Stefanik asked them.[39] Their response? In the words of CNN, the answers were 'opaque' and 'legalistic'.[40] It depends on 'the context', they said.[41] Such genocidal utterances might be 'investigated as harassment' if they were 'pervasive and severe', said Kornbluth of MIT. We would take action if such speech were to 'cross… into conduct', said Gay of Harvard.[42] I guess it was a relief to know that these citadels of learning will take action against students who cross the line from talking about genocide to trying to carry one out.

And there you had it. University officials who in recent years had sat back as cancel culture ran riot on their campuses, as feminist believers in biology were harassed and black critics of identity politics were sidelined, were suddenly interested in 'context', in the importance of weighing things up, even if the thing being weighed up is Hitlerite dreaming of a Jewish genocide. Suddenly, wrote Anthony L Fisher at the *Daily Beast*, there was a 'new appreciation' for 'nuance'. The presidents' borderline nonchalant attitude towards genocide chat flew 'completely in the face of long-standing campus policies surrounding speech codes and microaggressions', said Fisher. Worse, it smacked of discrimination. The overnight rediscovery of the importance of context 'isolates Jews', said Fisher. It lowers them to a 'singular identity group' for whom the normal 'rules and protections of campus safetyism don't apply'.[43]

Such righteous concern for the exclusion of Jews from the 'safe space' was widespread in the aftermath of the Congressional hearing and following the surge of anti-Semitic hatred on 'progressive' campuses. 'Not another word – ever – about safe spaces, microaggressions or "erasure" on a college campus', said Robert Pondiscio of the American Enterprise Institute upon witnessing the 'safe space' mob undermine the safety of Jews: 'Not one more damn word.' 'Everyone gets a "safe space" at Columbia University... except Jews', said a distressed professor at the Columbia Business School.[44] 'Where is the safe space for Jews?', demanded one observer.[45]

These are reasonable questions. That Jews on campus are so forcefully expelled from the 'safe space', that they are denied the protections of political correctness afforded to black students, Muslim students, trans students and others, is flagrant bigotry. In the early 20th century there was an unacknowledged 'Jewish quota' that limited the numbers of these supposedly problematic people who were permitted to attend universities like Harvard. Now there is a baldly stated 'Jewish quota' for how many of 'them' can enter the safe space and be forcefielded from slurs about Poland and chants for the destruction of their national homeland: that is, *none*. No Jew enjoys access to this sacred zone.

And yet, the worst possible response to this prejudicial treatment, to this branding of Jews as undeserving of the comfort blanket of 'progressive' care, would be to call for a more uniform, 'just' application of campus speech codes. The worst response to the barring of Jews from the 'safe space' would be to demand a more equitable 'safe space', for one and all, in which non-Jew and Jew alike might sink into a beanbag, grab a fistful of Play-Doh, and escape the slings and arrows of testy discussion. The worst response to the pogrom's exposure of the inherent bigotries in campus safetyism would be to call for the expansion of campus safetyism to include Jews, too.

No, the solution is not to have a more egalitarian 'safe space' but to dismantle the ideology of the safe space entirely. The true fairness we need in the modern university is not the fair inclusion of Jews in the systems of psychic protection, but the exclusion of all students from such gravely infantilising policies. Far from demanding the right of entry for Jews into this culture that reduces students to the level of overgrown children who require 24/7 shielding from sore words and hard ideas, we should demand the liberation of all from this ideological trap in which the price of 'safety' is your autonomy. The safe space's bar on Jews might be fuelled by bigotry, but there's a compliment hidden in the racism: Jewish students, for whatever reason, are seen as capable of withstanding the harshness of life outside the safe space. It is now time to trust that other students, too, have this capacity for moral independence.

The key reason that expanding 'progressive' ideologies on campus would be worse than useless for dealing with the rise of anti-Semitism is that these ideologies are *responsible* for the rise of anti-Semitism. The safe-space ideology, the politics of identity, the omnipresent campus policy of DEI (diversity, equity and inclusion) – these things are the fuel of the new Jew hate, of the 'progressive' racism that infected the Anglo-American academy after 7 October.

It was these ideologies' ruthless sorting of every ethnic group according to their 'privilege' or 'oppression' that led to the fresh targeting of Jews. It was their construction of an unforgiving moral narrative in which certain groups are historically oppressed, and thus must be afforded recognition and resources, while others are historically privileged, and thus must atone and apologise, that made Jews the ultimate outgroup. Viewed as white – 'hyper-white', in fact[46] – and privileged, viewed as the ultimate 'colonisers', Jews are the Emmanuel Goldsteins of the DEI ideology. The 'progressive' retribution against Jews was summed up by reports of an event at Stanford University a week after the 7 October pogrom. A lecturer called on Jewish and Israeli students to 'identify themselves'. They were then made to stand in a corner where they were subjected to a lecture on 'what Israel does to Palestinians'.[47] Lining Jews up for public shaming? It is remarkable how much the new 'anti-racism' mimics the old racism.

The DEI ideology drives this dehumanisation. DEI is the organisational framework of virtually every campus in the West. It is presented as a pro-equity regime whose aim is to foster a culture of fairness, especially for historically underrepresented groups. But in truth, it's a racial sorting mechanism that favours certain groups at the expense of others. As writer Sean Collins says, the DEI ideology treats people as 'monolithic embodiments of their racial, sexual and other identities, rather than as individuals'. It attends to the needs of so-called 'marginalised' groups but it has no room for 'Asians, whites and Jews' – the privileged – 'who are viewed with suspicion if not outright hostility by DEI advocates'.[48]

It fuels animosity 'towards Jews specifically', says Collins. They are the super-privileged in the eyes of DEI's 'schematic racial hierarchy'. What's more, DEI practitioners are expressly hostile to Israel, viewing it as a 'genocidal, settler-colonialist state'.[49] With its painting of Jews as the beneficiaries of historical privilege, and of the Jewish homeland as uniquely problematic, it was all but inevitable that in the arenas in which this neo-racialist ideology holds sway, Jews would come under attack. University administrators might wring their hands over the menacing of Jews on their campuses since 7 October, but it was their own racialisation of campus life, their own instituting of an ideology that accords or denies moral worth depending on an ethnic group's presumed levels of privilege, that hung a target sign around Jews' necks.

In a sense, then, it is not a double standard at all that Jews are excluded from the protections of political correctness. It is not a *failing* of this ideology that means this ethnic group in particular enjoys none of its flatteries or validations. No, it is consistent with a system of racial sorting and racial preference that some racial groups will be elevated and others demoted. It makes sense that an ideology designed to reprimand the privileged 'races' and assist the oppressed 'races' would so ruthlessly 'other' a group like the Jews. It is inevitable that a cultural elite drunk on a new politics of race that splits us into camps marked 'oppressed' and 'oppressor' – which is to say, worthy and unworthy – would come to sympathise with certain groups and despise others.

In his sharp polemical critique of the modern left's blind spot on the Jews, on the Jews' exclusion from the 'sacred circle' of progressive concern, David Baddiel says it is clear that 'Jews don't count'.[50] I'm not sure that's right. It seems to me that Jews count for a great deal in modern progressive activism. They matter enormously. Their role is huge. It's the role of oppressor, of coloniser, of *threat*. Jews, arguably, are the lead actors in the identitarian melodrama, having been allotted the part of the hyper-problematic. They are the oppressor against whom the oppressed might rage, the colonisers whom the just must 'decolonise'. The rage against Jews on campuses since 7 October suggests Jews matter rather too much to the emergent new elites, who clearly view them as the embodiment of white, Western arrogance that every decent DEI acolyte must chide and tame.

Post-7 October, we witnessed just how violent the supposed 'safe space' can be. We saw the ugliness and intolerance of this new ideology of censorship. It became clear that in the very act of promising students protection from supposedly transgressive people, the safe space also puts those transgressive people in the crosshairs, exposing them to severe forms of both social and physical reprimand. In the very act of depicting certain ideas as a threat to your entire sense of self, as the potential eraser of your whole identity, the safe space incites fear, hatred and even violence towards those ideas. And, by extension, towards the people who hold them. The rise of racism, intolerance and brutality on 'progressive' campuses after 7 October confirms that when you educate the young to fear difference and disagreement, you encourage them to hate those who are different and those who disagree.

The best pushback against this carnival of bigotry is a full-throated defence of the thing that both the pogromists and their Western sympathisers hate: freedom. Freedom of conscience, freedom of thought and freedom of speech. That might mean a world where people are free to say 'Kill all Jews', but it also means a world where many more of us are free to say: 'No. Never again.'

ENDNOTES

[1] Resources on Implicit Bias & Microaggressions, George Washington University

[2] Glory to our martyrs' projected onto building at George Washington University, *Times of Israel*, 26 October 2023

[3] Resources on Implicit Bias & Microaggressions, George Washington University

[4] Terrorist-loving GWU students 'honor' Hamas 'martyrs' and call to 'globalize the Intifada', *Campus Reform*, 26 April 2024

[5] George Washington University Is Moving on From 'Colonials', *New York Times*, 26 March 2023

[6] 'People Don't Want to Talk About It', *GW Today*, 18 February 2015

[7] Laura Kipnis calls out the 'feminine passivity' of rape culture in *Unwanted Advances*, *Chicago Reader*, 24 April 2017

[8] Laura Kipnis calls out the 'feminine passivity' of rape culture in *Unwanted Advances*, *Chicago Reader*, 24 April 2017

[9] A 'Left-Wing Feminist' Attacks the Climate of Sexual Paranoia on Campus, *National Review*, 24 April 2017

[10] The Campus Rape Culture That Never Was, *Minding the Campus*, 11 February 2019

[11] The Campus Rape Culture That Never Was, *Minding the Campus*, 11 February 2019

[12] Why the Campus Protests Are So Troubling, *New York Times*, 8 May 2024

[13] Elite schools turning into Hamas University as antisemitism runs rampant, *New York Post*, 22 April 2024

[14] Pro-Palestine protesters swarm *New York Times* for reporting Hamas rapes, *Jewish Chronicle*, 15 March 2024

[15] Palestinian Youth Movement, NGO Monitor, 2 June 2024

[16] Pro-Palestine protesters swarm *New York Times* for reporting Hamas rapes, *Jewish Chronicle*, 15 March 2024

[17] Pro-Palestine protesters swarm *New York Times* for reporting Hamas rapes, *Jewish Chronicle*, 15 March 2024

[18] Thirty-one Harvard organizations blame Israel for Hamas attack: 'Entirely responsible', *New York Post*, 9 October 2023

[19] Harvard Student's Op-Ed: Our School's 'Safe Space' Isn't Safe Enough, *National Review*, 2 April 2015

[20] UK universities' Gaza camps: Crafting in drizzle and pints at the pub, *The Times*, 2 May 2024

[21] Students revolt as union bans Eminem, *Guardian*, 2 February 2001

[22] Universities ban Blurred Lines on campuses around UK, *Guardian*, 20 September 2013

[23] Students Protest Sommers' Lecture, *Oberlin Review*, 24 April 2015

[24] Students Are Literally 'Hiding from Scary Ideas,' Or Why My Mom's Nursery School Is Edgier Than College, *Reason*, 22 March 2015

[25] Cambridge University's animals help students de-stress, BBC News, 20 May 2018

[26] Jack Russell brought into Cambridge University to help students de-stress left exhausted after he's booked for hours of walks, *Sun*, 14 May 2018

[27] Cambridge Uni students get Shakespeare trigger warnings, BBC News, 19 October 2017

[28] Campus Antisemitism Is Making Free Speech Fashionable Again, *Psychology Today*, 11 December 2023

[29] 'Pigs of the earth'? Don't you dare call this anti-Zionism, *Australian*, 24 April 2024

[30] Thousands at Washington pro-Palestinian protest, with some chanting 'Intifada' and rushing White House fence, Jewish Telegraphic Agency, 5 November 2023

[31] 'Pigs of the earth'? Don't you dare call this anti-Zionism, *Australian*, 24 April 2024

[32] Examples of Verbal and NonVerbal Microaggressions, City of Cambridge Mayor's Office, Massachusetts

[33] Elite schools turning into Hamas University as antisemitism runs rampant, *New York Post*, 22 April 2024

[34] Jewish UPenn student describes frightening antisemitic campus culture: 'They want to obliterate us', *New York Post*, 10 November 2023

[35] Horror as GWU protester carries sign with Nazi 'final solution' call for extermination of Jews, *New York Post*, 26 April 2024

[36] Terrified Jewish students flee campus after abuse from 100-strong mob, *Jewish Chronicle*, 7 March 2024

[37] Elite schools turning into Hamas University as antisemitism runs rampant, *New York Post*, 22 April 2024

[38] Protest Forces Cancellation of Milo Yiannopoulos Event at UC Berkeley, KQED, 1 February 2017

[39] Why Ivy League universities are so blasé about genocide, *spiked*, 6 December 2023

[40] After Harvard and Penn president resignations, focus of ire shifts to MIT's Kornbluth, CNN, 3 January 2024

[41] US uni presidents say calls for Jewish genocide might be allowed 'depending on context', *Jewish Chronicle*, 6 December 2023

[42] Why Ivy League universities are so blasé about genocide, *spiked*, 6 December 2023

[43] The Hamas-Israel War Obliterated the Campus Microaggression, *Daily Beast*, 9 December 2023

[44] Columbia Assistant Professor: "Everyone gets a "safe space" at Columbia University. Everyone, that is, except Jews", CTECH, 19 October 2023

[45] Where Is the Safe Space for Jews?, *Washington Stand*, 23 April 2024

[46] *Israelophobia: The Newest Version of the Oldest Hatred and What To Do About It*, Jake Wallis Simons, Constable, 2023

[47] Stanford professor suspended for calling Jewish students 'colonisers', *Jewish Chronicle*, 13 October 2023

[48] You can't beat anti-Semitism with 'diversity' training, *spiked*, 20 November 2023

[49] You can't beat anti-Semitism with 'diversity' training, *spiked*, 20 November 2023

[50] *Jews Don't Count*, David Baddiel, TLS Books, 2021

EIGHT

THE PURGE

A truly startling thing occurred on 8 October 2023: professors warmed to the pogrom. Some even seemed to view it as their theories put into practice, as a bloody, explosive extension of their own life's work. As smoke still billowed from the scarred terrain of southern Israel, as bodies were waiting to be collected, there were academics in the West claiming to see *themselves* in this violent outrage. In the broken, blackened warzone made by the fascists of Hamas, they saw, not a crime against humanity, but a physical manifestation of their own way of thinking. In Hamas's barbarism they glimpsed their own ideas made scorching flesh. There's a name for what happened in Israel over the past 24 hours, they said: it's 'decolonisation'.

'Decolonisation' was the word on the lips and tweeting fingertips of many academics and students in the hours and days after Hamas's savagery. Now we can see, said a researcher at the London School of Economics, that 'decolonisation is not a metaphor'. It doesn't just mean decolonising the curriculum, he said, referring to the fashionable academic cause of cleansing universities of their supposed overreliance on 'white, Western' thought and 'white, Western' writers, and opening them up to the influence of Indigenous thinkers, too. No, decolonisation is also physical, *violent*. It also means the 'resistance of the oppressed', he said, and 'that includes armed struggle'.[1]

The insistence that 'decolonisation is not a metaphor' could be heard everywhere following the pogrom. It was emblazoned on placards on student demonstrations. As a writer for the *Jerusalem Post* said, attend any 'pro-Palestine' demo at a US university and you're 'likely to see someone carrying a sign reading "Decolonisation is not a metaphor".'[2] Almost immediately after the pogrom, the Students for Justice in Palestine chapter at George Washington University issued a statement praising Hamas's assault and declaring: 'Decolonisation is NOT a metaphor.'[3]

Two academics at the University of Sussex in the UK repeated the cry, 'Decolonisation is not a metaphor'. The events of 7 October were 'horrifying', they said in a co-authored piece, but let's not forget the 'crucial backdrop': 'Israel's settler-colonial project.'[4] A professor at St Lawrence University in New York got snarky with his colleagues. 'If you think "decolonisation" is fine for your syllabus, your curriculum, or your classroom, but not for actual colonised people in Palestine, then you've never understood decolonisation', he barked: 'Please stop using the term until you take the time to educate yourself.' An academic in queer studies at Paris Cité University issued a similar diktat: 'All scholars who've even once used the term "decolonisation" for the advancement of their careers, please note that now is the time to show solidarity with Palestine.'[5]

Other thinkers were even more forthcoming with their admiration for Hamas's strike and what a boon it was for decolonisation. 'The sight of the Palestinian resistance fighters storming Israeli checkpoints separating Gaza from Israel was astounding', wrote Joseph Massad, professor of modern Arab politics and intellectual history at Columbia University in NYC.

It inspired 'jubilation and awe', he said.[6] The grand old man of the British left, Tariq Ali, said Palestinians had broken out of their 'open-air prison' and, in the face of an indifferent 'Western civilisation', were 'rising up against the colonisers'.[7] This was published on 7 October itself. The bodies of the murdered Israelis – who he called 'colonisers' – were barely cold.

Others stated the thesis more boldly. What Hamas did in southern Israel, they said, was a continuation of the things *we* do in our universities. It was an armed expression of ideas we ourselves hold. It was our 'decolonisation' theories given brute force. 'Postcolonial, anticolonial and decolonial are not just words you heard in your [DEI] workshop', said a professor at McMaster University in Canada. Journalist Najma Sharif distilled the thinking in a tweet that went viral in the hours after Hamas's bloodshed. 'What did y'all think decolonisation meant? Vibes? Papers? Essays?', she asked. Then a one-word insult for those who did think this, who did think 'decolonisation' was a cool crusade to get more non-white writers on the syllabus and not also extreme butchery of civilians: 'Losers.'[8]

Something extraordinary was happening here. Something that demands reflection. Academics were rushing to be associated with one of the most disturbing acts of violence of modern times. Members of our educated classes – professors, lecturers, writers – were effectively saying of Hamas's pogrom: 'That's my research in action.' As author Doug Stokes put it, they saw this slaying of Israelis as 'decolonisation in action'; they justified 'the sadistic actions of an ultra-bigoted, anti-Semitic group of Islamists in terms of "decolonisation"'.[9] It's almost like they were taking responsibility, intellectually at least. Hamas might have taken military responsibility for the slaughter, rape and kidnap of Jews. But the educated of the West were staking a claim to moral responsibility. *What did y'all think decolonisation meant?* It meant this, apparently. It meant violence against those branded 'colonisers'. It meant 'decolonising' the Earth of their toxic presence. It meant death.

That some in our educated classes welcomed Hamas's atrocity as a kind of armed wing of their own thinking was telling indeed. It spoke to a connection, at some level, between an intellectual anti-humanism in the West and the militant anti-humanism of Hamas. It spoke to a bond, however informal, between our own elites' straying from the virtues of civilisation and Hamas's violent disregard for civilisation. And it spoke to the sinister nature of what is called 'decolonisation'. If this vogue theory beloved of the West's professors, teachers, museums, art galleries and activist classes means not only replacing Geoffrey Chaucer with Alice Walker, but also murdering Jewish people, then we have a very serious problem.

'Decolonisation' is the buzzword of our times. Everyone's at it. University reading lists are being decolonised. Philosophy is being decolonised. Music is being decolonised. Museums are being decolonised. Science is being decolonised. Even brains are being decolonised. In his seminal 'decolonisation' text of 1986, *Decolonising the Mind*, Kenyan post-colonial theorist Ngũgĩ wa Thiong'o said we must free our minds from the 'false universalism' of 'Western forms of knowledge'.[10] This has been the goal of the academic crusade of decolonisation ever since – to loosen the hold of 'Western knowledge' in our institutions and schools and embrace alternative, apparently better ways of thinking about everything from the human condition to the scientific method.

The meaning of the word 'decolonisation' has morphed dramatically over the decades. As Joanna Williams writes, it was once used to refer to 'the period following the Second World War', when 'formerly colonised countries, primarily in Africa, sought independence'. In that context, 'decolonisation was an important practical and political process', writes Williams.[11] The D-word described the processes through which once subjugated nations moved towards national autonomy, towards something like democracy following decades of foreign rule. The *Oxford English Dictionary* describes decolonisation as 'the withdrawal of a colonising state from its colonies, leaving them independent'; decolonisation is 'the acquisition of political or economic independence'.

Not anymore it isn't. Now it means something else entirely. Now it means not the freeing of foreign nations from imperial control, but the freeing of our own institutions from their overdependence on Western knowledge, the Western canon and Western philosophy. Now it means not the liberation of African or Asian nations from the distant oversight of the West's colonialists, but the liberation of a new generation in the West itself from the baleful influence of 'whiteness' in their school and university curricula and in every museum and gallery they're likely to visit. Now it means not forcing out the foreign rulers of India, Angola, Kenya and too many other countries to mention, but forcing out Kant, Milton and even Aristotle from the world of education on the basis that students have had too much of such 'whiteness' and should now be exposed to 'the wealth of wisdom from Africa, Asia, the Middle East, Latin America and Indigenous communities'.[12]

This urge to rinse the world of learning of 'Western knowledge' is widespread. There is barely an educational or cultural institution left that has not embraced 'decolonisation' in some form; that is not now in thrall to this impulse to 'expand the perspectives they portray beyond those of the dominant cultural group, particularly white colonisers', as the *Washington Post* favourably describes it.[13] In some arenas it has become a holy crusade, something akin to an intellectual exorcism. Student activists across the West cry, 'Decolonise the curriculum!'. Students at Yale demanded the 'decolonisation' of the English syllabus, the sidelining of Shakespeare and Chaucer, on the basis that it is 'unacceptable that a Yale student considering studying English literature might read only white male authors'.[14] Some universities in the UK are likewise 'moving away' from Shakespeare and Chaucer in an effort to 'liberate their courses from "white, Western and Eurocentric" knowledge'.[15] More universities 'must decolonise', thundered a writer for the *Guardian*: 'Our teaching has to go beyond elite white men.'[16]

No subject is safe from the cudgels of decolonisation. The School of Oriental and African Studies (SOAS) in London has a 'decolonise philosophy' movement devoted to replacing the 'white' thought of Aristotle and Socrates with more novel thinking, including that of a 'Nigerian gender theorist' and a 'Japanese zen expert'.[17] Aristotle, the founding father of the Western philosophical tradition, frequently gets it in the neck from the marauding decolonisers of the modern campus. That he thought slavery was natural – as did everyone in Ancient Greece – is proof he held 'heinous views', says a professor of philosophy at Vassar College in the US, and so must be cast into suspicion. We must 'remember that among our students are people who have felt firsthand the continuing practical consequences of Aristotle's more heinous views', he says.[18] In short, ethnic-minority students of the present might feel aggrieved by some of the thinking of this man from the past.[19]

Virtually every week, a great man – or a 'dead white man', as we must now refer to them[20] – is dragged before the kangaroo court of the decolonisers and found to have held views that we in the morally perfect 21st century consider unacceptable. In the words of Frank Furedi, 'Aristotle, Chaucer, Shakespeare, Hume and Kant' are 'hauled' before the decolonisation mob and 'charged with various cultural crimes'.[21] Immanuel Kant, the great German philosopher of the Enlightenment, felt the wrath of a UK student group called 'Decolonise our Minds', which wants him off the syllabus. 'They Kant be serious!', cried the *Daily Mail*.[22] David Hume, the godfather of the Scottish Enlightenment, has suffered the indignity of having his name scrubbed from public buildings, so atrocious, apparently, were his 'cultural crimes'. Edinburgh University renamed its David Hume Tower in 2020 over Hume's 'comments on matters of race'.[23]

The decolonise urge often takes the form of erasing 'problematic' people from the public realm. A woke mob's toppling of the statue of 17th-century merchant and slave-trader Edward Colston, in Bristol in England in 2020, was celebrated by one historian as the 'decolonisation' of the public square.[24] For years, students at Oxford University demanded 'Rhodes Must Fall', in reference to a statue of 19th-century British colonialist Cecil Rhodes in Oriel College. Ridding Oxford of this likeness of Rhodes was not just about 'tearing down an outward symbol of British imperialism', we were told – it was also about 'confronting the toxic inheritance of the past'.[25] So, decolonisation is a kind of purification, a zealous reckoning with the supposed sins of Western history, with the 'toxic' hangovers of our so-called civilisation.

Some decolonisers go so far as to liken problematic monuments to acts of violence. One of the Oxford crusaders against the Rhodes statue said, 'There's a violence to having to walk past the statue every day on the way to your lectures... there's a violence to having to sit with paintings of former slave-holders while writing your [essays]'.[26] There are decolonise activists in the West who expressed far greater fury over old statues of long-dead men than they ever did over images of freshly killed women from Hamas's terror against the Jews.

The decolonise drive is ceaseless. The UK Museums Association has signalled its backing of 'Decolonisation in Museums', insisting these citadels of civilisation 'reappraise their own historical role in Empire'.[27] The Science Museum in London has discussed 'Decolonising Science'.[28] Yes, even science has been got at. Even this reasoned method for understanding nature and discovering truth is being disrupted by decolonise zealots. Perhaps it's time, posits one theorist of decolonisation, that we interrogated Western science's arrogant claim to be 'objective, solely empirical [and] immaculately rational'.[29] Very few ideals of the Enlightenment have been spared the dismantling instincts of the decolonise mob.

What it all adds up to is an assault on the gains of Western civilisation itself. The founding principles of Western philosophy, the discovery of the scientific method, the Enlightened thought of Kant and Hume, even the music of Beethoven (his Fifth Symphony is an offensive symbol of 'white male superiority and importance', apparently[30]) – all the ideas and culture that are the building blocks of our civilisation are feverishly targeted by the decolonisers. They co-opt the progressive language of 20th-century anti-colonialism to dress up an agenda that is entirely *regressive*. They appropriate past wars for liberation to add a veneer of radicalism to their own wars against culture and truth. As Christopher McGovern of the UK's Campaign for Real Education says, 'decolonisation' is fundamentally a 'code for erasing the identity and extraordinary achievements of Western civilisation.'[31]

And now we start to understand why some of the decolonisers glimpsed their own ideological crusading in the deranged crusading of Hamas on 7 October. Why they used their sacred word – 'decolonisation' – to describe Hamas's assault on Israel. Why they considered it to be 'decolonisation in action.'[32] For isn't Hamas's ideology also a profoundly reactionary one that disguises itself in the language of 'national liberation'? Doesn't Hamas likewise wage war on all that is good and call it 'anti-colonialism'? Isn't Hamas also an enemy of civilisation, a loather of Western modernity and its achievements, envisioning its violence as a means of purifying itself and its world of such toxic, foreign influences? The thin line, intellectually at least, between the 'decolonising' campaigns of the West's cultural elites and the 'decolonising' violence of Hamas should leave us cold.

Some really did feel an association, even a bond, with what unfolded in Israel on 7 October. As one columnist described it, there were 'writers and academics' who were 'very keen to *associate* the violence... with "decolonisation".'[33] Slavoj Žižek likewise noted that Hamas's attack 'was perceived by many [in the West] as an attempt at actual decolonisation.'[34] Some cited it as proof that decolonisation is both an important process of cleansing Western institutions of the influence of 'white colonisers' *and* violent struggle against 'settler colonialism'.[35] In the words of a professor in Middle Eastern studies at the University of California, Irvine, Hamas's act of 'mass violence' should jolt us into recognising that we need the 'decolonisation of our collective future'. That is, decolonisation for everyone: 'Decolonisation not just in Israel / Palestine, but globally, before the violence engulfs us all.'[36] So, Hamas will 'decolonise' the Middle East, and we must continue 'decolonising' the West.

One thing ought to be clear: when Western thinkers and agitators speak of 'decolonisation' in relation to Gaza and Hamas, what they're talking about has nothing to do with the decolonisation that took place following the Second World War. It has nothing in common with the anti-colonial struggles of that period and the undoing of colonial structures that occurred in African nations and elsewhere in the global South. The Israel / Palestine question does not remotely map on to those earlier acts of decolonisation. For two reasons. First, Israel is not, in fact, a settler-colonial nation. And second, Hamas is not a national-liberation movement. Far from it.

The depiction of Israel as a nation born of 'European settler colonialism', as the world's one remaining example of racist Europeans dominating a foreign people, is false. The modern state of Israel was forged not from colonialism but from *anti*-colonialism. Yes, in the 1920s and 1930s, the British Colonial Office occasionally acted favourably towards the Jews of what was then British-ruled Mandatory Palestine. But it was fundamentally the uprising of Jewish revolutionaries against the British rulers, an uprising that raged from 1944 to 1948, that ensured the end of Britain's mandate and the creation of the Jewish State. As Jake Wallis Simons says, the truth is that 'the manner of [Israel's] creation was typical of the period'. Like many other nations itching for freedom from the Empire in the wake of the Second World War, Israel fought for its national independence and was 'established legitimately under international law after the withdrawal of Imperial Britain'.[37]

The irony of the 'decolonise' set's loathing for Israel above all other nations is that Israel is a *decolonised* nation. The Jewish State went through the actual process of decolonisation, when, like other aspirant states of the postwar era, it established its independence from the Empire and 'replaced Western institutions with more democratic forms of government'.[38] The irony is too much: Israel has contributed far more to the ideal of decolonisation – its true ideal, that is, of seeking liberty from external diktat and unjust rule – than have any of its privileged haters in the West who think binning their copy of *Critique of Pure Reason* strikes a daring blow against 'white colonisers'.

As to the 'decolonise' movement's damning of Israel as 'white', as a 'white supremacist' pox on the true natives of that part of the world, this, too, is false. In fact, in the words of Simon Sebag Montefiore, the 'whiteness trope' that is 'key to the decolonisation ideology' is, if anything, 'more preposterous than the "coloniser" label'. In truth, Israel has a significant population of Ethiopian Jews. What's more, as Montefiore points out, around half of Israelis, close to five million people, are Mizrahi: 'descendants of Jews from Arab and Persian lands, people of the Middle East'. Why did the Mizrahi Jews end up in the Jewish State? Because after 1948 they were driven out of their homes in Baghdad, Cairo and Beirut where they had lived for 'many centuries, even millennia'.[39] To depict non-white Jews who were expelled from their ancestral lands by the hostile militia of Arab armies as 'colonisers' is an outrage against the historical record

If the decolonisers' branding of Israel as a white settler colony is false, their treatment of Hamas as anti-colonial is outright deluded. Hamas is as far from the anti-colonial movements of the postwar period as it is possible to get. Where those old movements aspired, at least, to represent 'the people', Hamas conceives of itself as an instrument of God. Where the anti-colonial movements of old swore themselves to creating a democratic state – even if many fell far short of that lofty goal – Hamas's dream is a theocratic state. And where the postwar anti-colonial struggles justified themselves in the language of anti-racism, insisting that non-whites were as capable as whites of governing their affairs, Hamas is an expressly racist organisation. Its aspiration is not racial equality but racial destruction. Its founding charter committed it to the obliteration of the Jews. As recently as April 2023, Hamas-linked preachers were sermonising for the 'paralysis' and 'annihilation' of the Jews – sermons Hamas fighters made good on with their massacres of 7 October.[40]

In the words of Daniel Ben-Ami, it is clear, 'from its own statements and activities', that Hamas 'is openly committed to the mass murder of Jews'. And there is 'no excuse for the left's ignorance about [these] genocidal aims'.[41] To brand Israel the embodiment of the racist and even genocidal thinking of European settler colonialism, and Hamas as the potential liberators of 'Historic Palestine', is a double calumny. It drips with ignorance about Israel's founding, and with suicidal naivety towards Hamas's true intention:

the creation of an unforgiving Caliphate in which Jews would not exist and women, gay people, leftists and trade unionists would suffer savage repression.

The decolonisers' view of Israel / Palestine represents a grotesque inversion of morality and truth. The state founded through an anti-colonial struggle is branded 'colonialist', while a movement devoted to the racist slaughter of Jews is called 'anti-colonialist'. The diverse people of a democratic nation are denounced as 'white supremacists', while the intolerant Jew-haters of Hamas are looked upon as freedom fighters. The people who were attacked by genocidal terrorists on 7 October are sneered at as 'genocidal', while their attackers are excused. 'Palestinian retaliation is wholly inevitable and entirely justifiable', as one British leftist said of this carnival of fascistic violence.[42]

If it is a distortion of historic levels to depict Hamas's pogrom as an act of 'decolonisation', why do so many in our cultural establishment insist on doing just that? Partly, they are deluding themselves. They are so ensnared by dinner-party prejudices that view Israel as uniquely wicked and the Palestinians as uniquely oppressed that they seem impervious to truth and reality. There is an element of desperate political yearning, too. To these self-styled radicals who inhabit the hallowed but dull halls of the Western academy, whose only act of revolutionary fervour was replacing Jane Austen with Toni Morrison on their course reading list, 7 October felt *exciting*.[43] It felt real. Like a revolt. It seemed to add the weight of world-historical violence to their drab campaigns of decolonisation. For all its death, it gave their politics life. And so they have a vested interest in not thinking about it in depth, and not believing all the details of what Hamas did, or they might discover that the price of their fleeting feeling of relevance was a thousand dead Jews.

There is something else, too. There's an ideological parallel, a moral connection, between the Western elites' urge to decolonise institutions and Hamas's urge to kill Israelis. It might be unspoken, and at times difficult to see, but it's there. Both represent a rage against civilisation. Both are fundamentally revolts against humanity. Both are rejections – one academic, one violent – of the awe and authority of culture. Where our decolonisers seek to 'erase the extraordinary achievements of Western civilisation', Hamas seeks to erase what it views as Western civilisation's imposition in the Middle East: Israel.[44] The cultural elites' instinct in the wake of 7 October to 'associate the violence' with their own theorising spoke to a recognition on their part of a truth they are unlikely to ever state out loud – Hamas's assault on the Jews mirrors their own assault on history.[45]

We should not be surprised. Since the 1970s, there has been a coming together of the West's postmodern left and radical Islamists, around a shared scepticism, and at times outright hostility, towards the moral and cultural claims of the West. There has been a 'confluence of contemporary radical Western and Islamist thought', as Sir John Jenkins describes it. And it is 'plain', he says, that 'both grew out of the same milieu [of] the revolt against Enlightenment rationality'. Radical Islam has more and more resonated 'with the European and American left precisely because it claims to have the same targets': the 'universalist claims of a Eurocentric and humanist modernity'.[46] A 'left', in particular in academia, that had lost faith in the virtues and truths of the Enlightenment felt ever more enticed by Islamist groups that likewise view the modern West as a false god.

This new 'confluence' was captured in the elation of philosopher Michel Foucault following Iran's Islamic Revolution of 1979. Foucault's work is hugely influential in 'decolonisation' circles. He is described as 'one of the patron saints of critical theory'.[47] He visited Tehran twice during the revolution and felt 'dazzled' by this 'revolt of the subaltern'. He hailed its deliverance to the world of a new 'political spirituality'.[48] Rather less was said about the revolution's disastrous consequences, for political freedom, regional peace and women. Forty years of critical theory later, four more decades of the deeper descent of the Western academy into the pit of post-Enlightenment, and now we hear positive noises even for an out-and-out pogrom. Even for something more degraded, more inhuman, than the revolution Foucault foolishly cheered. History repeated as farce, courtesy of the cultural establishment's ongoing rejection of the reason and rationalism that were modernity's gifts.

Decolonisation is decivilisation. It is a purge. It is the purging of our institutions of the ideas and ideals that shaped our societies. It is a secular jihad: the attempted eradication of the gains of modernity by a cosseted elite that has decided it has no more use of them. That some in this elite viewed the pogrom of 7 October as a visceral extension of their theories suggests decolonisation is dehumanisation, too. Even that Jews, in that hated state of Israel, symbolise, in some way, the sins of Western civilisation that these decolonisers wish to wash away. Perhaps, to paraphrase Heinrich Heine, where one 'decolonises' books, one will soon 'decolonise' people. And Hamas has made it clear what 'decolonising' people looks like.

For centuries, Jews have been seen as the harbingers of unsettling modernity. In the words of the historian of the Jews, Michael A Meyer, they were considered 'the very symbols of modernity'. They were often held 'collectively responsible for fostering values that destroyed the medieval consensus and substituted a society of alienated individuals for an earlier harmonious community'.[49] In short: they provoke, they wreck, they drag man into new, disorientating worlds. This racist fear has returned. You see it in the depiction of the Jews as the authors of our bloodthirsty neoliberalism. And as the inflictors of violent Europeanism on the native land of an Arab people. And as 'colonisers' without compare. Once more they are the disruptors of 'harmony', and therefore war must be waged against them, with pogroms in Israel, and physical assaults in the West, and the punishment of them for their privilege in the academy.

Today's war on Jews is a war on humanity. It is a war on civilisation. It is a violent manifestation of our societies' turn against the values of modernity and the wisdom of Enlightenment. It is a war that the 'decolonisers', of both the West and the Middle East, absolutely must lose.

ENDNOTES

[1] Decolonisation is not a metaphor, it is violence, Laura Dodsworth Substack, 9 October 2023

[2] How 'decolonization' became the latest flashpoint in the discourse over Israel, *Jerusalem Post*, 4 December 2023

[3] How 'decolonization' became the latest flashpoint in the discourse over Israel, *Jerusalem Post*, 4 December 2023

[4] *Contextualising Gaza: Colonial Violence and Occupation*, Institute of Development Studies, 13 October 2023

[5] Canadian academics shrug at horrendous violence perpetrated against Israelis, *National Post*, 11 October 2023

[6] The Professors and the Pogrom: How the theory of 'Zionist Settler Colonialism' reframed the 7 October massacre as 'Liberation', *Fathom*, November 2023

[7] Uprising in Palestine, *New Left Review*, 7 October 2023

[8] The dangers of 'decolonisation', *spiked*, 28 October 2023

[9] The dangers of 'decolonisation', *spiked*, 28 October 2023

[10] *Decolonising the Mind: The Politics of Language in African Literature*, Ngũgĩ wa Thiong'o, James Currey, 1986

[11] Against decolonising the curriculum, CIEO, 7 March 2024

[12] Aristotle and Socrates are sidelined as woke academics try to 'decolonialise' philosophers taught in classrooms and rely less upon 'dead white men' - with new-age thinkers including a Nigerian 'gender theorist' and Indian-American feminist, *Daily Mail*, 13 June 2024

[13] The 'decolonization' of the American Museum, *Washington Post*, 12 October 2018

[14] Yale English students call for end of focus on white male writers, *Guardian*, 1 June 2016

[15] Universities drop Chaucer and Shakespeare as 'decolonisation' takes root, *Telegraph*, 22 August 2022

[16] Yes, we must decolonise: our teaching has to go beyond elite white men, *Guardian*, 27 October 2017

[17] Aristotle and Socrates are sidelined as woke academics try to 'decolonialise' philosophers taught in classrooms and rely less upon 'dead white men' - with new-age thinkers including a Nigerian 'gender theorist' and Indian-American feminist, *Daily Mail*, 13 June 2024

[18] Cancel Culture Is Undermining Learning and Harming Students like Me, FEE, 17 August 2020

[19] Should We Cancel Aristotle?, *New York Times*, 21 July 2020

[20] Aristotle and Socrates are sidelined as woke academics try to 'decolonialise' philosophers taught in classrooms and rely less upon 'dead white men' - with new-age thinkers including a Nigerian 'gender theorist' and Indian-American feminist, *Daily Mail*, 13 June 2024

[21] *The War Against the Past*, Frank Furedi, Polity Books, 2024

[22] Are Soas students right to 'decolonise' their minds from western philosophers?, *Guardian*, 19 February 2017

[23] Edinburgh University renames David Hume Tower over 'racist' views, BBC News, 13 September 2020

[24] Toppling Colston: decolonisation of our own practice, *On History*, 29 April 2022

[25] *Rhodes Must Fall: The Struggle to Decolonise the Racist Heart of Empire*, Brian Kwoba et al, Bloomsbury Publishing, 2018

[26] Oxford Students Want 'Racist' Statue Removed, Sky, 12 July 2015

[27] Supporting Decolonisation in Museums, Museums Association

[28] See Decolonising Science Narratives conference, Science Museum, 2019

[29] Decolonizing Science and Science Education in a Postcolonial Space, Sage Journals, March 2016

[30] Classical Music's Suicide Pact, *City Journal*, Summer 2021

[31] Plan by woke academics to 'decolonise' philosophy by sidelining Aristotle and Socrates in favour of new-age thinkers is 'erasing extraordinary achievements of Western civilisation', say campaigners, *Daily Mail*, 13 June 2024

[32] The dangers of 'decolonisation', *spiked*, 28 October 2023

[33] Decolonisation is not a metaphor, *Critic*, 9 October 2023

[34] What the left gets wrong about Gaza and 'decolonisation', *New Statesman*, 20 December 2023

[35] Decolonisation is not a metaphor, it is violence, Laura Dodsworth Substack, 9 October 2023

[36] 'From the river to the sea' and the decolonisation of our collective future, Al Jazeera, 15 November 2023

[37] *Israelophobia: The Newest Version of the Oldest Hatred and What To Do About It*, Jake Wallis Simons, Constable, 2023

[38] Against decolonising the curriculum , CIEO, 7 March 2024

[39] The Decolonization Narrative Is Dangerous and False, *Atlantic*, 27 October 2023

[40] Hamas in Its Own Words, ADL, 10 January 2024

[41] This is not about 'liberating' Palestine, *spiked*, 9 October 2023

[42] This is not about 'liberating' Palestine, *spiked*, 9 October 2023

[43] Jane Austen replaced on literature course by American author Toni Morrison to 'decolonise' curriculum, *Wales Online*, 6 April 2022

[44] Aristotle and Socrates are sidelined as woke academics try to 'decolonialise' philosophers taught in classrooms and rely less upon 'dead white men' - with new-age thinkers including a Nigerian 'gender theorist' and Indian-American feminist, *Daily Mail*, 13 June 2024

[45] Decolonisation is not a metaphor, *Critic*, 9 October 2023

[46] *Islamism and the Left*, Policy Exchange, December 2021

[47] *Islamism and the Left*, Policy Exchange, December 2021

[48] *Islamism and the Left*, Policy Exchange, December 2021

[49] Modernity as a Crisis for the Jews, Michael A Meyer, *Modern Judaism*, Vol 9, No 2, May 1989

NINE

THE BLOOD OF ZIONISTS

When an Islamic activist on the streets of west London, a stone's throw from the Israeli Embassy, cried out 'We want the Zionists, we want their blood', who was he talking about? It was May 2021. There had been a noisy anti-Israel demonstration. A gang of men were barking insults at the Jewish State through their megaphones. It's a 'terrorist apartheid state', they cried. 'We will get our vengeance', they promised. Then one of the gang was heard lusting for Zionist blood. Was this just a political statement, if an angry, violent one? Was he merely referring to people who adhere to the Zionist belief that the Jews have the right to their own homeland? Might he have been referring to Gentiles as well as Jews who believe Israel has a right to exist?

When, in March 2024, someone scrawled the words 'Zionism = Nazism' on the wall of a synagogue in Norwich, England, was that political commentary?[1] Political commentary where it shouldn't have been, sure, but political commentary nonetheless? Was it an unwisely placed expression of an *idea* – namely, that the nationalism known as Zionism is problematic?

How about when the private home of Anne Pasternak, the Jewish director of the Brooklyn Museum, was doused in red paint in June 2024 before a sign was hung in her doorway calling her a 'white supremacist Zionist'?[2] Was that just moral judgement of a woman's presumed political beliefs? Was it an ill-advised act of protest at a private dwelling, not unlike when pro-choice activists gathered outside the home of the pro-life Supreme Court justice, Brett Kavanaugh, to let him know that they think his views on abortion stink? That is, was it dumb, but political?

How about when keffiyeh-wearing protesters got on the New York City subway in June 2024 and one of them shouted, 'Raise your hand if you're a Zionist'?[3] How about when his comrades then echoed his words, in that robotic, amplifying style beloved of the modern left, meaning that on a crowded train in New York City there was a large group of people loudly calling on Zionists to identify themselves? How about when the protesters, some of whom were wearing masks, then informed any Zionist who might have been lurking in the carriage that 'this is your chance to get out'? How about when, with no Zionist forthcoming, they said: 'Okay, no Zionists here, we're good'? Was that political agitation? Was it a simple request, if a menacing one, that the adherents of an ideology – the ideology of Zionism – go away? Was it confrontational political activism?

How about when, in the wake of 7 October, students at UCLA daubed 'Death to Zionism' on the wall of their library?[4] Or when the words 'Free Palestine, Fuck Zionists' were scrawled on a bus stop in Homerton in east London? Or when students at Birmingham University unfurled a banner saying, 'Zionists off our campus'?[5] Or when an Amazon employee scrawled 'Death to Zionists' on a scrap of paper and put it inside a book about Israel that he was shipping to a customer?[6] Or when a pro-Palestine protester in London waved a placard saying, 'The BBC is an arm of the Zionist propaganda machine'?[7] Or when student protesters in America displayed banners saying, 'End Zionism'?[8] Or when a protester in Washington, DC waved a placard saying, 'Zionism is a cancer to this planet'?[9] Or when someone in New York wrote 'Zionism is terrorism' on a poster showing one of Hamas's kidnap victims?[10] Or when a British MP was called 'Zionist scum' online?[11] Or when one of the organisers of the Gaza encampment at Columbia University in NYC said 'Zionists don't deserve to live'?[12]

Was it all politics? Colourful, rude, offensive and at times downright bitter, yes, but still politics? Straight condemnation of a doctrine and those who support it? After all, these people did not use the word 'Jew'. They did not say 'Fuck Jews', 'Jewish scum' or 'Raise your hand if you're a Jew'. They said 'Fuck Zionists', 'Zionist scum' and 'Raise your hand if you're a Zionist'. They didn't tell Jews to get off the subway; they told Zionists to get off the subway. They didn't say Jews are ugly; they said Zionists are ugly. They didn't say Judaism is a cancer to the planet; they said Zionism is a cancer to the planet. It's totally different. The former would be racial hatred, no question. The latter is brash, irksome and threatening, for sure, but it's political criticism. Political criticism of a form of nationalism, of a style of government, of a belief.

Right?

Of course not. And anyone still seeking to maintain this illusion – this illusion that 'anti-Zionism is not anti-Semitism', this fantasy that criticism of Israel is no different to criticism of any other country – is kidding themselves.[13] One thing made painfully clear in the fallout from 7 October is that 'anti-Zionism' is the mask anti-Semitism now wears. That opposing Zionism is the veil behind which Jew hate hides. That when people say 'Zionist', very, very often they mean Jew. The ugliness, the hysteria and the boiling animus in the hate for the world's only Jewish nation clearly does not belong to the realm of political criticism or political protest, but rather to that ancient universe of fear and loathing for one people and one people only.

We know for a fact that some of the events mentioned above were venomous acts of race hate masquerading as political protest. For instance, that Islamist in west London who gave voice to his desire for Zionist blood also said: 'We'll find some Jews here!'[14] Clearly, the Z-word and J-word are interchangeable in the new fascism. One of his fellow 'protesters' pointed at his trainers, which seemed to have mini Israel flags on them, and said: 'This is the Nike anti-Jewish edition.' So, this was a Jew-hunt in the guise of a protest against Israel. It was a brewing pogrom that pretended its target was Zionism.

As to the scrawling of 'Zionism = Nazism' outside the Norwich Synagogue – pure race hate. It had it all: it was an attack on Jews' place of worship; it taunted Jews with the word 'Nazism', with memories of their people's extermination; it implied racial guilt, as if all Jews bear responsibility for Israel's every act. To add insult to racist injury, Norwich has the dubious honour of being the city in Europe where the anti-Semitic blood libel first emerged. It was 1144. The Jews of Norwich found themselves accused, with not a sliver of evidence, of the ritual murder of a 12-year-old boy called William in order that they might drain his blood.[15] A calumny was born and it spread like a pox through Europe, with similar accusations issued everywhere, leading to pogroms, expulsions and untold death.[16] Anti-Semites in Norwich might now say 'Zionist' rather than 'Jew' but their belief that this people is uniquely bloodlusting seems undimmed.

And the attack on Anne Pasternak's home? That took place in the wake of a 'Day of Rage for Gaza' in New York City on 10 June 2024. There had been protests against the 'Nova Exhibition NYC' on Wall Street, an art-installation-cum-tribute to the victims of 7 October. Anti-Israel protesters damned the exhibition as 'Zionist propaganda' and said it was 'manufacturing consent for genocide'. In Union Square, protesters unfurled a banner saying 'Long Live 7 October'. 'Not even "Free Palestine" or "Palestine from the River to the Sea"', said one observer, 'but long live a day of death, destruction, rage and abduction aimed almost solely at civilians.'[17] It was a breakaway group of agitators from this 'Day of Rage' who went on the subway hunting for 'Zionists'. And later some of them visited Ms Pasternak's home to splash it with red paint and damn her as having 'blood on her hands'.

Let us be frank: this was a pogrom disguised as a 'Day of Rage'. It was a Jew hunt dressed up as a Zionist hunt. When you are protesting against an exhibition honouring the victims of modern-day fascism, and singing the praises of Hamas's anti-Jewish savagery of 7 October, and searching the subway for 'Zionists', and descending on the homes of 'Zionists', you are not engaging in political protest – you are engaging in a modern version of an ancient violence, a pogrom under the cover of the Palestine colours. As Nora Berman wrote of the 'Day of Rage': 'It is now clear all manner of anti-Semitic sins can be indulged under the guise of opposing Zionism.'[18]

And the other incidents, the other chants? When people say the

BBC, and the rest of the media, is an 'arm of the Zionist propaganda machine', we all know what they mean. We all know they are rehabilitating the vile old belief that the Jews control the media, and just about everything else, though they give it a bit of PC spit and polish by saying 'the Zionists' rather than 'the Jews'. When people say 'Zionism is a cancer to the planet', we all hear the echoes of old hatreds that depicted Judaism as a disease-like scourge on Earth. We all hear the reverberations of the old Nazi view of Jews as lice, as the spreaders of typhus, as essentially a 'deadly contagious disease'.[19]

And when people say 'Zionists off our campus', 'End Zionism', 'Death to Zionism', 'Fuck Zionists' and 'Zionists are ugly', the question has got to be: why? Why are they so enraged by this one form of national politics? By *this* idea of nationhood above all others? Why have they never gone out in public to demand death for Lithuanian nationalists, for instance? Or to damn Italian nationalists as ugly and cancerous? Or to say 'fuck you' and 'please die' to people who believe in Turkish statehood? Why is it only Zionism that boils their piss and makes them want to take to the streets and even has them swarming public transport in an unhinged hunt for those who subscribe to this idea of statehood? The very potency of the rage against Zionism, the singular, furious nature of it, is an indictment of its bigotry and irrationalism. Its very 'language of loathing', as Howard Jacobson calls it, which is 'passed from the culpable to the unwary and back again', makes clear that this febrile agitation bubbles up from far darker wells than 'politics'.[20]

Anti-Zionism is racism. There may be interesting critiques of Zionism, genuine analytical interrogations of it, worthwhile probings of both its theory and its practice. Certainly, that kind of questioning existed historically, and it often came from Jews. But all of that has been overshadowed, utterly, by an anti-Zionism that contains little more than a frothing, violence-tinged antipathy for one nation, and by extension for one people. At that protest outside the 'Nova Exhibition NYC', there was a protester holding a sign that said Zionists are 'not humans'.[21] There it was. The dehumanisation of the Jews. The robbing, once more, of their humanity. The return of the fascist imagination.

Zionism, plainly put, is the belief that Jews have a right to a nation in their ancestral homeland. The word Zion comes from the Bible. It's a reference to the mountain in Jerusalem where King David is thought to be buried. Over the millennia, as Jewish historian Suzanne Rutland describes it, 'Zion' came to 'refer to Jerusalem itself, as well as the Land of Israel'. The word *Zionism*, the name given to the movement for Jewish national self-determination, did not emerge until the 1890s, when Theodor Herzl, the father of political Zionism, injected the project of Jewish statehood with real moral and political momentum.[22] Though, of course, as Jake Wallis Simons says, the dream of a Jewish return to Israel long predated the 19th century – there was a 'unique ancientness', he writes, to the Jews' 'yearning for a return to their homeland'.[23]

For all the rage against Zionism as a uniquely malign dream of statehood, as a kind of ethno-hysteria that marks it out as the worst and most evil of nationalisms, in truth it is akin to other longings for national independence. Yes, the 'ancientness' of the Jews' dreams of Zion, combined with their experience of 'centuries of appalling persecution', meant the Zionist project had some distinctive features, says Wallis Simons. But fundamentally, in the tumult of the turn of the 20th century, 'Zionism was not unusual': 'It was simply one expression of the nationalism that arose as the empires of the Ottomans, Austro-Hungarians, Russians and eventually the Western powers gave way to new nation states from the end of the First World War onwards.'[24]

The argument put forward by critics of Israel is that because Zionism is a political project, criticism of it is political, too. Opposition to it is political. Even hatred for it is political. It is not racist, they say, to raise objections to a political idea. As Adam Serwer wrote in the *Atlantic*, 'Political Zionism, defined concisely, is the belief that the Jews should have a Jewish state in their ancestral homeland. Anti-Zionism, in similarly brief terms, is the opposition to that belief.' It should not be a surprise, he says, that Palestinians and their Western sympathisers are 'anti-Zionist'. There is 'nothing anti-Semitic' about believing 'the existence of a religious or ethnically defined state is inherently racist', Serwer says.[25] Others insist that criticism of Israel is not anti-Semitic, and that saying that it is can come across as a sly attempt to 'silence critics of Israel's occupation.'[26]

In a boring way, these commentators are right. Criticising Israel – saying, for example, that you don't approve of its wars, or you don't like its food, or you find it too hot – is not racist, clearly. But what we see on our streets and campuses and in our newspapers day in, day out is not 'criticism of Israel' – it is steaming hatred for Israel. It is not a political critique of Zionism – it is the damnation of Zionism as uniquely malevolent, as bloodthirsty, as a lethal menace not only to Palestinians, but also to the entirety of humankind. It is not anti-war – it is anti an entire nation state whose destruction is openly longed for, campaigned for, gloried over. 'We don't want no two states / We want '48!' It isn't a simple cry for 'Hands off Gaza', like the cries of 'Hands off Vietnam' or 'Hands off Ireland' we heard in the past. No, it is a rally, a worldwide rally, a curiously hotheaded rally, for the shaming, punishment and possibly even the death of Zionism.

Show me one other anti-war movement of recent times that has campaigned not only for an end to war, but also for an end to a *country*. Which has not only accused a nation of carrying out an unjust military campaign, but has also accused it of being a cancer, 'uniquely murderous', psychotic, a threat to all mankind.[27] Which has marshalled with such glee the spectre of Nazism. Which has described the nation it opposes not only as wrong or wicked, but also as genocidal, Hitler-like, intent on dragging the people it 'oppresses' into a hell not unlike the Warsaw Ghetto.[28]

This is not criticism – it is hysteria. It is not opposition – it is hatred. It is not even denunciation – it is a death sentence for Jewish nationalism and Jewish nationalism alone. Those who say criticising a country and an ideology is not racist are technically right but historically naive. They fail to grasp what is new and distinctive about the 'criticism' of Zionism in the 21st century. They fail to understand the very unusualness of the sight of millions of people around the world not only opposing Zionism but also *defining themselves* by their opposition to it. That people call themselves 'anti-Zionist', that this proud, angry negation of the idea of Jewish nationhood is such a central feature of their political belief system and social identity, is itself a red flag. Criticising Israel might not be racist, but arranging your entire personality around an obsessive, rancorous hatred for Israel is, well, questionable, if we're going to be kind.

The historical context of today's 'anti-Zionism' must always be taken into consideration. Of course there have been many instances in history where people have criticised the Zionist project. Many of the critics were Jews. In the 20th century there were Jews who expressed both religious and political opposition to the idea of Zionism. The religious criticism centred on a belief that a Jewish State should not be built until the Messiah comes, and then it should be a theocratic state, not a state like all the others.[29]

The political criticism, much of it coming from Jewish Marxist revolutionaries, centred on the conviction that to separate the Jews from Gentile societies by creating for them their own homeland represented an *accommodation* with anti-Semitism rather than a challenge to it. To remove ourselves from society would be to let the pogromists win, Leon Trotsky and others argued. Of course, this view held far less sway following the Nazi mania of the 1940s, when it became clear that the Jews' survival as a people was now wholly in question. The ancient dream of returning to Zion became a matter of exceptional urgency following the enslavement and extermination of the Jews by the Nazis and their local allies.

Israel will be a 'bloody trap' for the Jews, Trotsky famously said. 'Zionism is incapable of resolving the Jewish question', he argued.[30] Rosa Luxemburg, the German revolutionary who was also Jewish, was likewise sceptical of the early claims of Zionism. But here's the thing: she equally fumed against other nationalisms. She wrote, in her inimitable style, against the nationalism of the Poles, too, and the Ukrainians, the Lithuanians, the Czechs. 'Ten new nations of the Caucasus... rotting corpses [that] climb up out of hundred-year-old graves... and feel a passionate urge to form states', she thundered.[31] She was anti-nationalist, not anti-Zionist. Hers was an even critique of nationalist movements, not a one-eyed despising of Jewish nationalism alone. As Michael Walzer has argued, the striking thing about 'Luxemburg's loathing' was its 'universalism'. A feature, he says, that is 'missing from much contemporary leftism, where the loathing is much more limited'. What is striking today, says Walzer, is that the Jewish State, despite being 'very much like all the other states', finds itself on the 'receiving end of such a singular version of Luxemburgian loathing'.[32]

This is the key point. It is the singular nature of anti-Zionism, the myopia of its loathing, the intensity and outright ferocity of its focus on one nation and its founding ideals, that distinguishes it from past political and religious critiques of Zionism. That makes it feel new, unsettling, dangerous even. That makes it clear that the insistence of Israel's critics in the commentariat that 'Anti-Zionism is not anti-Semitism' just will not cut it anymore. To fail to grasp the historically specific character of modern anti-Zionism is to be wilfully blind at this stage. To fail to recognise its regressive features is to allow your own opposition to Israel to cloud whatever capacity for moral judgement you might have left. To fail to ask *why* – why the obsession, why the strength of feeling, why the hunt for Zionists on trains, campuses, streets – is to make yourself complicit in the re-emergence of old hatreds in new language.

Moreover, to fail to interrogate how 'anti-Zionism' managed to give a new lease of life even to the far right is unforgivable. Five minutes on the internet, less in fact, will make it clear that neo-fascists have rehabilitated their hateful ideologies in the language of 'anti-Zionism'. This has been gathering pace for some time. As historian Benjamin Bland has written, after the Second World War the 'extreme right' had a 'major obstacle standing in its way': 'The horrors of the Holocaust.' It was hard to be a fascist once everyone knew what fascism had wrought. So the extreme right adopted two tactics in the postwar decades. First, they denied the Holocaust had happened. And second, they embraced 'anti-Zionism' as a means of expressing their anti-Semitism. Anti-Zionism became, in Bland's words, 'a mask for their Nazi sympathies'.[33] If your 'criticism of Israel' gives life to fascistic extremists, then you need a reckoning with your 'criticism of Israel'.

What has happened is extraordinary: the self-styled anti-fascists of the cultural establishment have created the conditions for a resurgence of fascism. Fascism of both the hard-right and Islamist variety. In making hatred of the world's only Jewish nation a key barometer of moral and political worth, a central feature of their activism, their commentary and their art, the cultural elites have fashioned a terrain in which hatred for *Jews* has been able to flourish. In turning a blind eye to the anti-Semitic bigotries of radical Islamists, on the grounds that it is 'Islamophobic' to criticise people of the Islamic faith, they have given a green light to these people's racial animus, to their desire for 'Zionist blood'. In failing to reckon with the newness of today's 'anti-Zionism', and instead robotically insisting that 'it is not racist to criticise Israel', they have allowed the extreme right to reinvent itself as just another angry opponent of that most evil creed on Earth: Zionism.

The opinion-forming set, which for years denounced every

populist movement it disliked as 'far right', has now brought the actual far right back into public life. There they are on the internet, on our streets, lurking in areas with large Jewish populations, saying 'Death to Zionism', when what they really mean, and we all know it, is 'Death to Jews'.

For who are these 'Zionists' that the campus left, the radical commentariat, influencers, Islamists and neo-fascists hate so much? They are Jews. Three quarters of Britain's Jews feel a strong attachment to Israel. Sixty-three per cent of them identify as Zionist.[34] (Down from 72 per cent a decade ago, no doubt as a result of the cultural establishment's transformation of the word 'Zionist' into a byword for wickedness.) Surveys show that around 80 per cent of America's Jews are 'pro-Israel'.[35] In Australia, 77 per cent of Jews identify as Zionist, and 86 per cent agree that the existence of Israel is essential for the future of the Jewish people.[36] It's time to get real: when people say 'Fuck Zionists', they are saying 'Fuck Jews'.

What has happened, it seems to me, is that the old dread and prejudice for Jews is now projected on to the Jewish State. The old scapegoating of the Jews has been replaced by a scapegoating of Israel. The irrational fear people once felt towards Jews they now feel towards that place where many Jews live.

The belief in the uniquely murderous nature of Israel, the craven obsession with its spilling of the blood of Palestinian children, echoes the blood libels that spread from Norwich across Europe in the Middle Ages. The belief that Israel is all-powerful, that its lobby has mighty America and the UK eating out of the palm of its hand, mimics the old view of Judaism as a many tentacled beast, pulling strings everywhere. The claim that 'the Zionists' control the media is a new version of the old bigoted fear of awesome 'Jewish power'. And the idea that Israel is a cancer, a disease, an entity so terrible that it threatens world peace as well as Middle Eastern peace, has chilling echoes of the Nazi delirium that said the Jews were responsible for every ill, including Germany's economic torpor and political crisis.

'Anti-Zionism' is the form that Jew scapegoating takes in the 21st century. Where once people pinned their community's every trouble on the Jews in their midst, now people hold Israel responsible for the ills not only of the Middle East, but of the West, of the *world*, too. Where once people blamed their strife and misfortune, the seeming lack in their lives, on conniving Jews, now armies of Western radicals and Western youths find an explanation for their feelings of disorientation in the power and wickedness of Israel. They pin the sins of their societies, the sins of the world, on one nation. The Jewish nation. This is the irony of anti-Zionism: it is itself proof of why Zionism is necessary. The very hatred for Israel among the educated of the West shows why Israel must exist. No more justification for Israel's existence is necessary than the fact that so many wish to bring Israel crashing down.

The aftermath of 7 October exposed the irrationalism of Israelophobia. It confirmed that today's burning hatred for Israel is fundamentally a manifestation of the moral disarray and drift into unreason of the West itself. That's what anti-Zionism is: not a political critique of an idea, but the physical, intellectual, rancid embodiment of the West's own crisis of meaning. They say the sleep of reason brings forth monsters. Our sleep of reason has certainly done that. It has brought back the ideology of the pogrom, the imagination of fascism itself, into societies we dreamt were enlightened.

ENDNOTES

[1] 'Zionism is Nazism' scrawled on Norwich synagogue, *Jewish Chronicle*, 14 March 2024

[2] Vandals Splash Graffiti on Home of Jewish Director of Brooklyn Museum, *New York Times*, 12 June 2024

[3] When protests cross into antisemitism, it hurts the Palestinian cause, *Guardian*, 14 June 2024

[4] 'Are you a Zionist?' Checkpoints at UCLA encampment provoked fear, debate among Jews, *Los Angeles Times*, 9 May 2024

[5] Birmingham uni activists call for 'Zionists off our campus', *Jewish Chronicle*, 9 February 2024

[6] Amazon worker who added 'death to Zionists' note to order is suspended, *Jewish Chronicle*, 20 December 2023

[7] Pro-Palestine protesters wave 'Zionists control the media' placards during London march, *Telegraph*, 3 February 2024

[8] Tensions high as pro-Palestinian protests spread at college campuses across US, Reuters, 30 April 2024

[9] Red Lines, *Daily Campus*, 16 November 2023

[10] Transformed into mist, *Intercept*, 28 November 2023

[11] Jewish MP tells staff what to do if there is an attempt on his life, *Telegraph*, 26 January 2024

[12] Columbia University says it has banned student protester who said 'Zionists don't deserve to live', NBC, 27 April 2024

[13] Don't Equate Anti-Zionism With Anti-Semitism, *Atlantic*, 3 November 2023

[14] Embassy protester demanded 'Jewish blood', *The Times*, 30 May 2021

[15] 'Zionism is Nazism' scrawled on Norwich synagogue, *Jewish Chronicle*, 14 March 2024

[16] Blood Libels throughout History, Holocaust Encyclopedia

[17] When protests cross into antisemitism, it hurts the Palestinian cause, *Guardian*, 14 June 2024

[18] Threatening Jews is now acceptable – so long as you call them Zionists, *Forward*, 14 June 2024

[19] Public Health Under the Third Reich, Experiencing History – Holocaust Sources in Context

[20] Let's see the 'criticism' of Israel for what it really is, *Independent*, 18 February 2009

[21] Threatening Jews is now acceptable – so long as you call them Zionists, *Forward*, 14 June 2024

[22] When does anti-Zionism become antisemitism? A Jewish historian's perspective, *Conversation*, 27 March 2024

[23] *Israelophobia: The Newest Version of the Oldest Hatred and What To Do About It,* Jake Wallis Simons, Constable, 2023

[24] *Israelophobia: The Newest Version of the Oldest Hatred and What To Do About It,* Jake Wallis Simons, Constable, 2023

[25] Don't Equate Anti-Zionism With Anti-Semitism, *Atlantic*, 3 November 2023

[26] Anti-Jewish hatred is rising – we must see it for what it is, *Guardian*, 11 August 2014

[27] Israel's War Psychosis, *Counterpunch*, 31 March 2024

[28] Despite backlash, Masha Gessen says comparing Gaza to a Nazi-era ghetto is necessary, NPR, 22 December 2023

[29] Anti-Zionism and Anti-Semitism, *Fathom*, October 2019

[30] On the Jewish Problem, Leon Trotsky, 1937

[31] Anti-Zionism and Anti-Semitism, *Fathom*, October 2019

[32] Anti-Zionism and Anti-Semitism, *Fathom*, October 2019

[33] Holocaust inversion, anti-Zionism and British neo-fascism: the Israel–Palestine conflict and the extreme right in post-war Britain, *Patterns of Prejudice*, January 2019

[34] Benchmark survey of British Jews finds strong attachment to Israel and decline in Zionist identity, Religion Media Centre, February 2024

[35] The fall and rise of Jewish American Zionism, *Jerusalem Post*, 1 October 2023

[36] When does anti-Zionism become antisemitism? A Jewish historian's perspective, *Conversation*, 27 March 2024

TEN

JEWISH LIVES MATTER

Imagine if the Battle of Cable Street took place in 2024. Imagine if this celebrated clash between Jews and their working-class allies on one side, and a fascist movement on the other, were to blow up in 21st-century Britain. What would happen?

The actual Battle of Cable Street took place in the East End of London in 1936. It was a revolutionary uprising by Jews, leftists and workers against the threat posed by the British Union of Fascists. The BUF was founded by Oswald Mosley in 1932. Mosley had been a Conservative MP before crossing the floor of the House of Commons to join the Labour Party. At the start of the 1930s, following a trip to Italy to meet Mussolini, he converted to the cause of fascism. And he won over many in high society. Leading journalists, a peer, friends of royalty and, notoriously, two of the aristocratic Mitford sisters joined his fascist crusade. One of the Mitfords – Diana – went the whole hog and married him, at the home of Joseph Goebbels in Berlin, with Adolf Hitler as guest of honour.

The people of the East End were rather less taken with Mosley's Mussolini tribute act. And they let it be known when the BUF announced its intention to march through the East End on 4 October 1936. The East End had a large Jewish population then. The BUF's planned parade, in which thousands of its backers would be on the streets in their Blackshirts, was viewed by many East Enders as an intolerable anti-Semitic provocation. So they decided to take action. Against the advice of both the Metropolitan Police and the Labour Party, who were concerned that a counter-demonstration to Mosley's march would give rise to lawlessness, the workers of east London plotted their fightback.

Their slogan was 'They shall not pass', an echo of the cry of the Spanish republicans who had risen up against Franco's nationalist coup earlier that year. The East End rebels set up barricades on Cable Street. They used an overturned bus, tables, chairs and paving stones to block the fascists' access. They gathered together makeshift weaponry – rocks, chair legs, rotten vegetables and even the contents of their chamber pots – to wield against both the fascists and the Met police officers who tried to dismantle the barricades and clear the street. Children were sent out to roll marbles under the hooves of police horses. An entire community had prepared itself for all-out battle against fascism, and in defence of Jews.

When the battle came, it was intense. Mosley marshalled around 5,000 Blackshirts. On the other side, behind the barricades, there were thousands: Jews, Irish dock workers, communists, anarchists, trade unionists. There followed some of the most ferocious hand-to-hand combat ever seen on the streets of Britain. Bricks were hurled at Mosley's car, sticks were wielded against his Blackshirts, stones were thrown at the police who supported the Mosley mob's right to parade down Cable Street. Hundreds were injured, many arrested. And the anti-fascists won. In the face of baton charges by horse-mounted officers and the violent menace of the Blackshirts themselves, the Jews and their allies were victorious. Mosley abandoned his plans and scurried back to central London.

The Battle of Cable Street is rightly celebrated as one of the great people's uprisings of the early 20th century. There is a mural of it in east London today. There are books, films, even a musical. Many Britons are proud that in the 1930s, Jews in east London who had fled the anti-Semitic pogroms of Russia and Eastern Europe in the late 1800s and early 1900s did not suffer the same violence and indignity at the hands of Mosley's mob. (Although, on the weekend after the Battle of Cable Street, east London was rocked by the Pogrom of Mile End, when 200 Blackshirts smashed the windows of Jewish shops and homes.) The Battle of Cable Street is seen by many as the street fight that foretold Britain's war on Nazi Germany, as the trailblazer of our future showdown with fascism, as early proof that this racist, inhuman ideology then moving through Europe might just come unstuck against Britain.

And yet, what if it were today? What if a fascist mob marched through a Jewish area of London in 2024? Would we see an uprising of resistance, a taking to the streets to see off the fascists and rally around their targets? I fear we would not. I fear such solidarity is all but impossible in the era of identity politics, intersectionality and progressive suspicion of 'Jewish privilege'. I fear today the Jews might be on their own – though hopefully joined by that smattering of the population that still appreciates that when anti-Semitism rears its head, society is in deep trouble.

This is how I think it would play out. Initially, liberals and the left would express concern with the fascists' planned march. They might even sign a Change.org petition calling on parliament to ban it, given their preference for the taming influence of state authority over the unpredictable force of people power. They might put an anti-fascist symbol in their social-media bio, next to their pronouns and the BLM fist. They would tweet 'Down with fascism' or 'Ban the march' and post a link to a *Guardian* article on the problematic history of fascism.

Soon, though, doubts would creep in. What about Islamophobia, some would say? Why all the focus on anti-Semitism? Why are we putting the suffering of the Jews at the top of 'the hierarchy of racism' *again*? An imagined 'hierarchy of racism' has been the obsession of Britain's left for years. They are convinced, in the absence of anything resembling evidence, that the Labour Party and other institutions of society prioritise sympathy for Jews above sympathy for other social groups. I don't think I have taken part in one media debate about anti-Semitism on the left without my interlocutor saying, 'And what about Islamophobia?'. It's like a tic they have.

Their intersectional beliefs would soon kick in. This is one of the most ruinous ideologies of the post-class left. It holds that the multiple forms of discrimination a group faces combine, overlap and 'intersect' to give rise to an entirely distinct experience of suffering that people from outside the group are unlikely to be able to understand. So where a Muslim woman, say, faces many 'intersecting' forms of discrimination – on the basis of her skin colour, her sex, her religious beliefs, her veil – a Jewish man experiences very few. He's white, he's male, he's probably cishet – he's *fine*. Intersectionality is motored by a toxic belief that some people are 'more oppressed' than others, and by extension that some people are 'more privileged'. How long would it be before the 'privilege' of the Jewish targets of the planned fascist march would become a factor in the discussion? Not very, I would wager.

Soon we would arrive at one of the higher, even more noxious stages of what passes for progressive discussion in the 2020s. Are the people being marched against Jews or Zionists, some would wonder? Do Israeli flags hang from the windows of the street the fascists intend to march on? If so, that might pose a problem. In fact, any outward Jewish symbol might be an issue for the modern activist class weighing up whether or not to take a stand against fascists. We've all seen the footage of a police officer in Scotland advising a Jewish man to hide his Star of David necklace lest it make pro-Palestine protesters 'very, very angry'.[1] We all remember when Gideon Falter of the Campaign Against Anti-Semitism walked by a pro-Palestine demo in London, in his kippah, and an officer advised him to move on. We all remember what the crowd chanted at Falter when he did move on: 'Zionist scum, Zionist scum, Zionist scum...'[2]

So, clearly, a judgement would need to be made before solidarity could be offered. Are these *Jew* Jews or Zionist Jews? Are they a little too proud of their Jewish identity, which might smack of Jewish chauvinism, and too supportive of Israel? If so, maybe *they're* the fascists? Perhaps they're the far-right threat? The progressive set's luxury belief of Israelophobia and its wariness of 'Jewish privilege', its tendency for viewing Jews who like Israel as bad Jews, might soon dampen its enthusiasm for going anywhere near that street where the fascists planned to march.

Then would come their most pressing, and ugliest, query. What do the fascists look like? If they were white-skinned and red-faced with beer bellies, a St George's flag wrapped round their shoulders, that might rekindle the interest of the activist class and the Smart Set in counter-protesting them. The post-class left loves a showdown with 'gammon'.[3] But if they were radical Islamists, if they were extremists who hail from a minority community, forget about it. No one wants to run the risk of being branded an Islamophobe. No one wants to compound the oppression of the supposedly oppressed by taking a stand against them. No one wants to be on the side of 'white' people against 'brown' people. Following this cruellest of calculations, this most regressive of deliberations, the modern Battle of Cable Street would be over before it had even begun.

And the denouement to this thwarted fight against fascism, to this fizzling out of a sequel to Cable Street? Perhaps one of the Jewish residents would post a video online tearfully asking where all the solidarity is. 'Okay, Karen', might come a reply. 'Cry harder, Zionist', someone might say. And, inevitably, *'What about Islamophobia?'*.

The Battle of Cable Street is inconceivable in modern Britain. The ideas, the bravery, the plain decency required for such a street fight with fascism no longer exist. The atomising creed of identitarianism, the relentless rise of privilege policing, the cult of competitive grievance, the wariness of Zionism that so often crosses over into wariness of Jews – all of this has ensured that those 20th-century gatherings across religious lines, colour lines and identity lines to fight for a greater, human cause are unrepeatable in the modern era. These poisonous political strains have made the Battle of Cable Street feel like a distant, almost ancient event. One we can admire but not really imagine. One that the cultural establishment romanticises while being blissfully unaware that were something similar to happen today, they wouldn't be on the side they think they would be on.

We don't even need to use our imaginations. Since 7 October we have seen with our own eyes what would happen if there were a sequel to Cable Street. We have seen liberals and leftists march shoulder to shoulder with radical Islamists calling for further pogroms against Jews. We have seen self-styled progressives mingle with Islamists chanting about Muhammad's violent vengeance against the Jews. We have seen bourgeois radicals chant 'Zionist scum' at a man in a kippah. We have seen left commentators make excuses for the bloodiest pogrom against the Jews since the Holocaust. And we have seen them say nothing when a man was given a paltry suspended sentence for threatening Jews with a knife in Golders Green in London.[4] And when three men in the north of England were arrested on suspicion of plotting a gun attack on Jews.[5] And when synagogues were attacked. And when Jewish schoolkids took off their blazers to dodge the attention of racists. And when anti-Semitic hate crimes in London rose by 1,350 per cent.[6]

Is silence still violence, as they told us during the BLM protests of 2020? If so, their 'violence' against Jews has been deafening.

The truth is that there have been mini Cable Streets in Britain and elsewhere almost every week since 7 October. Outbreaks of anti-Semitism, the mobbing of 'Zionist scum', the chanting for pogroms, the racist harassment of Jews on campus. And the left that loves what happened on Cable Street 90 years ago has either turned a blind eye or taken the side of the persecutors. This is the inhumanity of identity politics. This is where that post-class, hyper-racial, privilege-obsessed ideology of the cultural establishment ends up: with a low-level war on Jews, in broad daylight.

I cycled down Cable Street shortly after Hamas's pogrom. From virtually every lamppost there fluttered a Palestine flag. It's a mostly Muslim area now, the Jews having left long ago, so perhaps that is understandable. And yet I couldn't help but think how sad it is, how tragic even, that on this street where the Jews and their friends held back the tide of British fascism, there now flew the flag of the side that had just carried out a pogrom against the Jews, and not the flag of the side that suffered it.

A fightback is needed against the indifference of our elites to the difficulties facing Jewish people, and against their excuse-making for pogroms, and against their infliction on our societies of a politics of jealousy and division that they falsely call 'progressive'. And, most importantly, against the people on our streets agitating against 'Zionists', which means Jews. If you see them, tell them: You shall not pass.

ENDNOTES

[1] Police Scotland tell Jewish man to hide Star of David for 'safety', *Herald*, 14 February 2024

[2] What does a longer video of the exchange between Met officer and antisemitism campaigner tell us?, *Guardian*, 22 April 2024

[3] As Brexiteers and Right-wing voters are dismissed as 'gammon', BRENDAN O'NEILL reveals why Britain's elites hold ordinary people – and democracy – in such contempt, *Daily Mail*, 3 June 2023

[4] Why was this anti-Semitic maniac given a slap on the wrist?, *spiked*, 13 June 2024

[5] Three in court over alleged plot to attack Jewish community, BBC, 14 May 2024

[6] Antisemitic hate crimes in London up 1,350%, Met police say, *Guardian*, 20 October 2023

ABOUT THE AUTHOR

Brendan O'Neill is the chief political writer for *spiked*, based in London. He was *spiked*'s editor for almost 15 years, from 2007 to 2021. He hosts the weekly podcast, *The Brendan O'Neill Show*. His writing has appeared in the *Spectator*, the *Sun*, the *Daily Mail* and the *Australian*. His previous collections of essays include *A Heretic's Manifesto*, *A Duty to Offend* and *Anti-Woke*.

ABOUT SPIKED

spiked is the magazine that wants to change the world as well as report on it. Edited by Tom Slater, and launched in 2001, it is irreverent where others conform, questioning where others wallow in received wisdom, and radical where others cling to the status quo.

At a time when it is fashionable to cancel 'problematic' people, to sideline voters when they give the 'wrong' answer, and to treat human beings as a drain on the planet, we put the case for human endeavour, the expansion of democracy, and freedom of speech with no ifs or buts.

Our motto is 'question everything' – or as the *New York Times* put it, we are 'the often-biting British publication fond of puncturing all manner of ideological balloons'. Read us every day at spiked-online.com

Made in the USA
Middletown, DE
11 September 2025